ONLY
LOVE is
REAL

ONLY LOVE is REAL

The story of soulmates reunited

DR BRIAN WEISS

piatkus

PIATKUS

First published in the US by Warner Books, Inc., New York
First published in Great Britain in 1996 by Piatkus Books Ltd

A CIP catalogue record for this book
is available from the British Library.

ISBN 978-0-7499-1620-6

Designed by Giorgetta Bell McRee

Printed and bound in India by Manipal Technologies Ltd, Manipal

Papers used by Piatkus are from well-managed forests
and other responsible sources.

Piatkus
An imprint of
Little, Brown Book Group
100 Victoria Embankment
London EC4Y 0DY

An Hachette UK Company
www.hachette.co.uk

www.piatkus.co.uk

To Elizabeth and Pedro,
who have reminded me that there
are no coincidences in love

Leeza _Rajiv_

Happy Birthday Beb. ♡

Acknowledgments ────────────

My thanks for their constant love and support go to Carole, Jordan, and Amy.

My deepest appreciation goes to Joann Davis, my editor at Warner Books, for her encouragement, insight, and wisdom. She's the best.

I am indebted to Joni Evans, agent extraordinaire, for her boundless energy and enthusiasm.

And, finally, my gratitude goes to all of my patients and workshop participants, who have shared their lives with me.

*R*eader's Note _____

*P*sychiatrist-patient confidentiality is a strong and time-honored principle of psychiatric ethics. The patients mentioned in this book have authorized me to write their true histories. Only names and other identifying details have been altered in order to protect their privacy. Their stories are true and unchanged.

Preface

The soul of man is like to water;
From Heaven it cometh
To Heaven it riseth
And then returneth to earth,
Forever alternating.

GOETHE

*J*ust before my first book, *Many Lives, Many Masters*, was published, I visited the owner of a local bookstore to see if he had ordered it. We checked his computer.

"Four copies," he told me. "Do you want to order one?"

I wasn't very sure that sales of the book would ever reach the modest amount that the publisher had printed. After all, this was a very strange book for a respected psychiatrist to have written. The book describes the true story of a young patient of mine whose past-life therapy dramatically changed both our lives. However, I knew that my friends, neighbors, and, certainly, my relatives would buy more than four copies, even if the book didn't sell anywhere else in the country.

"Please," I said to him. "My friends, some of my patients, and other people I know will be coming here looking for my book. Can't you order more?"

I had to personally guarantee the one hundred books

he reluctantly ordered.

To my utter shock, the book has become an international bestseller with more than two million copies in print, and it has been translated into more than twenty languages. My life had taken another unusual twist.

After being graduated with honors from Columbia University and completing my medical training at the Yale University School of Medicine, I also completed an internship at New York University's teaching hospitals and a residency in psychiatry at Yale. Afterward, I was a professor on the medical faculties at the University of Pittsburgh and the University of Miami.

For the following eleven years, I was chairman of the Psychiatry Department at Mount Sinai Medical Center in Miami. I had written many scientific papers and book chapters. I was at the apex of an academic career.

Catherine, the young patient described in my first book, then walked into my office in Mount Sinai. Her detailed memories of past lifetimes, which I did not initially believe, and her ability to transmit transcendental messages while in a hypnotized trance state, turned my life upside down. I could no longer see the world as I had before.

After Catherine, many more patients came to me for past-life regression therapy. People with symptoms resistant to traditional medical treatments and psychotherapies were being cured.

Through Time into Healing, my second book, describes what I have learned about the healing potential of past-life regression therapy. The book is filled with true case stories of actual patients.

The most intriguing story of all is in *Only Love Is Real*, my third book. This book is about soulmates, people who are bonded eternally by their love and who come around together and together again, life after life. How we find and recognize our soulmates and the life-transforming decisions we must then make are among the most moving and important moments in our lives.

Destiny dictates the meeting of soulmates. We *will* meet them. But what we decide to do after that meeting falls in the province of choice or free will. A wrong choice or a missed chance can lead to incredible loneliness and suffering. A right choice, an opportunity realized, can bring us to profound bliss and happiness.

Elizabeth, a beautiful woman from the Midwest, began therapy with me because of her profound grief and anxiety after the death of her mother. She had also been having problems in her relationships with men, choosing losers, abusers, and other toxic partners. She had never found true love in any male relationship.

We began the journey back to distant times, with surprising results.

At the same time that Elizabeth was undergoing past-life therapy with me, I was also treating Pedro, a charming Mexican who was also suffering from grief. His brother had recently died in a tragic accident. In addition, problems with his mother and secrets from his younger days seemed to be conspiring against him.

Pedro was burdened with despair and doubts, and he had no one with whom to share his troubles.

He, too, began a search into ancient times to seek solutions and healing.

Although Elizabeth and Pedro were in therapy with me during the same time period, they had never met each other, as their appointments were scheduled on different days of the week.

Over the past fifteen years, I have often treated couples

and families who have discovered present-day partners and loved ones in their past lives. Sometimes I have regressed couples who simultaneously and for the first time have found themselves interacting in the same prior lifetime. These revelations are often shocking to the couple. They have not experienced anything like this before. They are silent while the scenes unfold in my psychiatric office. It is only afterward, after emerging from the relaxed, hypnotic state, that they first discover they have been watching the same scenes, feeling the same emotions. It is only then that I also become aware of their past-life connections.

But with Elizabeth and Pedro everything was reversed. Their lives, and their lifetimes, were unfolding independently and quite separately in my office. They did not know each other. They had never met. They were from different countries and cultures. Even I, seeing them both separately and having no reason to suspect a link between them, did not make a connection. Yet they seemed to be describing the same past lifetimes with stunning similarity of detail and emotion. Could they have loved each other and lost each other across lifetimes? In the beginning, none of us was aware of the gripping drama that had already begun to unfold in the unsuspecting serenity of my office.

I was the first to discover their connection. But now what? Should I tell them? What if I were wrong? What about patient-doctor confidentiality? What about their current relationships? What about tinkering with destiny? What if a current life connection was not in their plans or even in their best interests? Would another failed relationship undermine both the therapeutic gains that they had made as well as their trust in me? It had been ingrained in me during my medical school years and subsequent psychiatry residency at the Yale University School of Medicine to do no harm to patients. When in doubt, do no harm. Both Elizabeth and Pedro were improving. Should I just let it go at that?

Pedro was finishing his therapy and would soon leave the country. There was an urgency to my decision.

Not all of their sessions, particularly Elizabeth's, are included in this book, as some sessions were not pertinent to their stories. Some were completely devoted to traditional psychotherapy and did not include hypnosis or regression.

What follows is written from medical records, transcripts of tapes, and memory. Only names and minor details have been changed to ensure confidentiality. It is a story of destiny and of hope. It is a story that happens silently every day.

On this day, someone was listening.

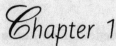
Chapter 1

Know, therefore, that from the greater silence I shall return. . . . Forget not that I shall come back to you. . . . A little while, a moment of rest upon the wind, and another woman shall bear me.

KAHLIL GIBRAN

There is someone special for everyone. Often there are two or three or even four. They come from different generations. They travel across oceans of time and the depths of heavenly dimensions to be with you again. They come from the other side, from heaven. They look different, but your heart knows them. Your heart has held them in arms like yours in the moon-filled deserts of Egypt and the ancient plains of Mongolia. You have ridden together in the armies of forgotten warrior-generals, and you have lived together in the sand-covered caves of the Ancient Ones. You are bonded together throughout eternity, and you will never be alone.

Your head may interfere: "I do not know you." Your heart knows.

He takes your hand for the first time, and the memory of his touch transcends time and sends a jolt through every atom of your being. She looks into your eyes, and you see a soul companion across centuries. Your stomach turns upside down. Your arms are gooseflesh. Everything outside this moment loses its importance.

He may not recognize you, even though you have finally met again, even though you know him. You can feel the bond. You can see the potential, the future. But he does not. His fears, his intellect, his problems keep a veil over his heart's eyes. He does not let you help him sweep the veil aside. You mourn and grieve, and he moves on. Destiny can be so delicate.

When both recognize each other, no volcano could erupt with more passion. The energy released is tremendous.

Soul recognition may be immediate. A sudden feeling of familiarity, of knowing this new person at depths far beyond what the conscious mind could know. At depths usually reserved for the most intimate family members. Or even deeper than that. Intuitively knowing what to say, how they will react. A feeling of safety and a trust far greater than could be earned in only one day or one week or one month.

Soul recognition may be subtle and slow. A dawning of awareness as the veil is gently lifted. Not everyone is ready to see right away. There is a timing at work, and patience may be necessary for the one who sees first.

You may be awakened to the presence of your soul companion by a look, a dream, a memory, a feeling. You may be awakened by the touch of his hands or the kiss of her lips, and your soul is jolted back to life.

The touch that awakens may be that of your child, of a parent, of a sibling, or of a true friend. Or it may be your beloved, reaching across the centuries, to kiss you once again and to remind you that you are together always, to the end of time.

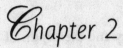

Chapter 2 _____

> My life as I lived it had often seemed to me like a
> story that has no beginning and no end. I had the
> feeling that I was a historical fragment, an excerpt for
> which the preceding and succeeding text was missing. I
> could well imagine that I might have lived in former
> centuries and there encountered questions I was not
> yet able to answer; that I had to be born again because
> I had not fulfilled the task that was given to me.
>
> CARL JUNG

Tall, thin, and attractive with long blonde hair, Elizabeth
had sad blue eyes with specks of hazel in them. Her
melancholy eyes overpowered her loose navy blue business suit as she sat nervously in the large white leather
reclining chair in my office.

Elizabeth felt compelled to see me, searching for hope
after reading *Many Lives, Many Masters* and identifying
with Catherine, the book's heroine, on many levels.

"I don't know much about why you're here," I commented, breaking the usual impasse at the beginning of
therapy. I had briefly glanced at the information sheet all
new patients fill out. Name, age, referral source, chief
complaints and symptoms. Elizabeth had listed grief, anxiety, and sleep disturbance as her major maladies. As she
began to talk, I mentally added "relationships" to her list.

"My life is such a mess," she stated. Her history began
to pour out, as if it were finally safe to talk about these
things. The release of pent-up pressure was palpable.

Despite the drama of her life's story and the depths of emotion lying just under the surface of her telling it, Elizabeth quickly minimized its importance.

"My story is not nearly as dramatic as Catherine's," she said. "There won't be any book about me."

Her story, dramatic or not, flowed forth.

Elizabeth was a successful businesswoman with her own accounting firm in Miami. Thirty-two years old, she was born and reared in rural Minnesota. She grew up on a large farm with her parents, an older brother, and many animals. Her father was a hard-working, stoical man who had great difficulty expressing his emotions. When he did display emotion, it was usually anger and rage. He would lose his temper and lash out impulsively at his family, sometimes striking her brother. The abuse Elizabeth received was only verbal, but it hurt her greatly.

Deep within her heart, Elizabeth still carried this childhood wound. Her self-image had been damaged by her father's condemnations and criticisms. A profound pain enveloped her heart. She felt impaired and somehow defective, and she worried that others, especially men, could also perceive her shortcomings.

Fortunately her father's outbursts were infrequent, and he quickly retreated to the stern and stoical isolation that characterized his personality and behavior.

Elizabeth's mother was a progressive and independent woman. She promoted Elizabeth's self-reliance while remaining warm and emotionally nurturing. Because of the children and the times, she chose to stay on the farm and to tolerate reluctantly her husband's harshness and emotional withdrawal.

"My mother was like an angel," Elizabeth went on. "Always there, always caring, always sacrificing for the sake of her children." Elizabeth, the baby, was her mother's favorite. She had many fond memories of childhood. The fondest of all were times of closeness to her mother, of the special love that bonded them together and that maintained itself over time.

Elizabeth grew up, was graduated from high school, and went away to college in Miami, where she had been offered a generous scholarship. Miami seemed like an exotic adventure to her, and she was lured away from the cold Midwest. Her mother reveled in Elizabeth's adventures. They were best friends, and even though they mostly communicated by phone and mail, their mother-daughter relationship stayed strong. Holidays and vacations were happy times for them, as Elizabeth rarely missed a chance to go back home.

During some of these visits, Elizabeth's mother talked about retiring to South Florida to be near Elizabeth. The family farm was large and increasingly difficult to run. They had saved a considerable amount of money, an amount augmented by her father's frugality. Elizabeth looked forward to living near her mother again. Their nearly daily contacts would no longer have to occur by telephone.

So Elizabeth stayed in Miami after college. She started her own accounting firm, which was slowly building. Competition was keen, and the work absorbed great chunks of her time. Relationships with men added to her stress.

Then disaster struck.

Approximately eight months prior to her first appointment with me, Elizabeth was devastated because of her mother's death from pancreatic cancer. Elizabeth felt as if her own heart had been torn apart and ripped out by the death of her beloved mother. She was having an enormously difficult time resolving her grief. She couldn't integrate it, couldn't understand why this had to happen.

Elizabeth painfully told me about her mother's courageous battle with the virulent cancer that ravaged her body. Her spirit and her love remained untouched. Both women felt a profound sadness. Physical separation was inevitable, quietly but persistently approaching. Elizabeth's father, grieving in anticipation, grew even more distant, wrapped in his solitude. Her brother, living in California with a young family and a new business, kept a physical distance. Elizabeth traveled to Minnesota as often as possible.

She had no one with whom to share her fears and her pain. She did not want to burden her dying mother any more than was absolutely necessary. So Elizabeth kept her despair inside, and each day felt increasingly heavy.

"I will miss you so much. . . . I love you," her mother told her. "The most difficult part is leaving you. I'm not afraid of dying. I'm not afraid of what awaits me. I just don't want to leave you yet."

As she grew weaker and weaker, her mother's resolve to stay longer gradually diminished. Death would be a welcome relief from the debility and the pain. Her last day arrived.

Elizabeth's mother was in the hospital, the small room crowded with family and visitors. Her breathing became erratic. The urine tubes showed no drainage; her kidneys had ceased to function. She lapsed into and out of consciousness. At one point Elizabeth found herself alone with her mother. At this moment her mother's eyes widened, and she became lucid again.

"I won't leave you," her mother said in a suddenly firm voice. "I'll always love you!"

Those were the last words Elizabeth heard from her mother, who now lapsed into a coma. Her respirations became even more erratic, with long stops and sudden, gasping starts.

Soon she was gone. Elizabeth felt a deep and gaping hole in her heart and in her life. She could actually feel a physical aching in her chest. She felt she would never be completely whole again. Elizabeth cried for months.

Elizabeth missed the frequent phone calls with her mother. She tried calling her father more often, but he remained withdrawn and had very little to talk about. He would be off the phone within a minute or two. He was not capable of nurturing or comforting her. He also was grieving, and his grief isolated him even more. Her brother in California, with his wife and two young children, was also devastated by his mother's death, but he was busy with his family and career.

Her grief began to evolve into a depression with increasingly significant symptoms. Elizabeth was having problems sleeping at night. She had difficulty falling asleep and she would awaken much too early in the morning, unable to fall back to sleep. She lost interest in food and began losing weight. She had a noticeable lack of energy. She lost enthusiasm for relationships, and her ability to concentrate became increasingly impaired.

Before her mother's death, Elizabeth's anxiety consisted mainly of job stresses, such as deadlines and difficult decisions. She was also anxious at times about her relationships with men, with how she should act and what their responses would be.

Elizabeth's anxiety levels increased dramatically after the death of her mother. She had lost her daily confidante and adviser, her closest friend. She had lost her primary source of guidance and support. Elizabeth felt disoriented, alone, adrift.

She called for an appointment.

Elizabeth came into my office hoping to find a past life in which she had been together with her mother or to contact her in a mystical experience. In books and lectures I have talked about people in meditative states having such mystical encounters with loved ones. Elizabeth had read my first book, and she seemed aware of the possibility of these experiences.

As people open up to the possibility, even the probability, of life after the death of the physical body, of the continuation of consciousness after leaving the physical body, they begin to have more of these mystical experiences in dreams and in other altered states of consciousness. Whether these encounters are real or not is difficult to prove. But they are vivid and filled with feeling. Sometimes the person even becomes aware of specific information, facts or details that were known only to the deceased. These revelations from spiritual visits are difficult to ascribe solely to imagination. I believe now that such new knowledge is obtained, or visits are made, not because people wish this to happen, not because they need it, but because this is the way contacts are made.

Often the messages are very similar, especially in dreams: I'm all right. I'm fine. Take care of yourself. I love you.

Elizabeth was hoping for some type of reunion or contact with her mother. Her heartache needed some balm to ease the constant pain.

More of her history emerged during this first session. Elizabeth had been married for a brief period of time to a local contractor, who had two children by a previous marriage. Although she was not passionately in love with this man, he was a good person, and she thought that this relationship would bring some stability into her life. But passion in a relationship cannot be artificially created. There can be respect, and there can be compassion, but the chemistry has to be there from the start. When Elizabeth discovered that her husband was having an extramarital affair with someone who could provide more excitement and passion, she reluctantly left the relationship. She was sad about the breakup and sad to leave the two children, but she did not grieve because of the divorce. The loss of her mother was much more severe.

Because of her physical beauty, Elizabeth found it easy to meet and date other men after the divorce. But none of these relationships had fire either. Elizabeth began to doubt herself, to try to find where within herself the fault lay in her inability to establish good relationships with men. "What is wrong with me?" she would ask herself. And her self-esteem would dip another notch.

The barbed arrows of her father's painful criticisms during her childhood had left wounds in her psyche. The failed relationships with men rubbed salt in these wounds.

She began a relationship with a professor at a nearby university, but he could not commit to her because of his own fears. Even though there was a strong feeling of tenderness and understanding, and even though the two communicated very well, his inability to commit to a relationship and to trust his feelings doomed that relationship to a quiet and unspectacular ending.

Some months later Elizabeth met and began dating a

successful banker. She felt secure and protected in this relationship even though, once again, the chemistry was limited. He, however, was strongly attracted to Elizabeth and became angry and jealous when she did not reciprocate with the kind of energy and enthusiasm that he expected. He began to drink more, and he became physically abusive. Elizabeth left this relationship, too.

She had been quietly despairing of ever meeting a man with whom she could have a good and intimate relationship.

She had thrown herself into her work, enlarging her firm, hiding behind the numbers and calculations and paperwork. Her relationships primarily consisted of business contacts. And even though from time to time a man would ask her out, Elizabeth would do something to discourage that interest before it grew into anything serious.

Elizabeth was aware that her biological clock was ticking, and she still hoped to meet the perfect man some day, but she had lost a great deal of confidence.

The first therapy session, devoted to gathering historical information, formulating a diagnosis and therapeutic approach, and sowing the seeds of trust in our relationship, had ended. The ice had been broken. I decided not to use Prozac or other antidepressants at this time. We would aim for a cure, not just the covering over of her symptoms.

At the next session, one week later, we would begin the arduous journey back through time.

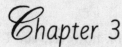

Chapter 3

So long ago! And yet I'm still the same Margaret.
It's only our lives that grow old. We are where
centuries only count as seconds, and after a thousand
lives our eyes begin to open.

EUGENE O'NEILL

*P*rior to my experiences with Catherine, I had never
even heard of past-life regression therapy. This was not
taught when I was at Yale Medical School, nor anywhere
else, I was to learn.

I can still vividly remember the first time. I had
instructed Catherine to travel backward in time, hoping
to discover childhood traumas that had been repressed,
or forgotten, and that I felt were causing her current
symptoms of anxiety and depression.

She had already reached a deeply hypnotized state,
which I had induced by gently relaxing her with my
voice. Her concentration was focused on my instructions.

During her therapy session the week previously, we
had used hypnosis for the first time. Catherine had
remembered several childhood traumas with considerable
detail and emotion. Usually in therapy, when forgotten
traumas are remembered with their accompanying emotions, a process called catharsis, patients begin to improve.

Catherine's symptoms remained severe, however, and I assumed that we had to uncover even more repressed childhood memories. Then she should improve.

Carefully I took Catherine back to the age of two, but she recalled no significant memories.

I instructed her firmly and clearly: "Go back to the time from which your symptoms arise." I was totally shocked by her response.

"I see white steps leading up to a building, a big white building with pillars, open in front. There are no doorways. I'm wearing a long dress . . . a sack made of rough material. My hair is braided, long blonde hair."

Her name was Aronda, a young woman who lived nearly four thousand years ago. She died suddenly in a flood or tidal wave, which devastated her village.

"There are big waves knocking down trees. There's no place to run. It's cold, the water is cold. I have to save my baby, but I cannot. . . . Just have to hold her tight. I drown; the water chokes me. I can't breathe, can't swallow . . . salty water. My baby is torn out of my arms."

Catherine had been gasping and having difficulty breathing during this tragic memory. Suddenly her body relaxed completely, and her breathing became deep and even.

"I see clouds. . . . My baby is with me. And others from my village. I see my brother."

She was resting. That lifetime had ended. Although neither she nor I believed in past lives, we had both been dramatically introduced to an ancient experience.

Incredibly, her lifelong fear of gagging, or choking, virtually disappeared after this one session. I knew that imagination or fantasy could not cure such deeply imbedded, chronic symptoms. Cathartic memory could.

Week after week, Catherine remembered more past lives. Her symptoms disappeared. She was cured, without the use of any medicines. Together, we had discovered the healing power of regression therapy.

Because of my skepticism and rigorous scientific training, I had a difficult time accepting the concept of past lives. Two factors eroded my skepticism, one rapid and highly emotional, the other gradual and intellectual.

In one session, Catherine had just remembered her death in an ancient lifetime, a death from an epidemic that had swept through the land. She was still in a deep hypnotic trance, aware of floating above her body, being drawn to a beautiful light. She began to speak.

"They tell me there are many gods, for God is in each of us."

She then began to tell me very private details about the lives and deaths of my father and my infant son. They had both died years previously, far away from Miami. Catherine, a laboratory technician at Mount Sinai Medical Center, knew nothing at all about them. There was no person who could have given her these details. There was no place to look up this information. She was stunningly accurate. I felt shocked and chilled as she related these hidden, secret truths.

"Who," I asked her, "who is there? Who tells you these things?"

"The Masters," she whispered, "the Master Spirits tell me. They tell me I have lived eighty-six times in physical state."

Catherine later described the Masters as highly evolved souls not presently in body who could speak to me through her. From them I received spectacular and profound information and insights.

Catherine had no background in physics or metaphysics. The knowledge the Masters transmitted seemed far beyond Catherine's capabilities. She knew nothing about dimensional planes and vibrational levels. Yet, deep in the trance state, she described these complex phenomena. Beyond that, the beauty of her words and thoughts and the philosophical implications of her utterings far transcended her conscious abilities. Catherine had never before talked in such a concise, poetic manner.

When I listened to her as she relayed concepts from the Masters, I could sense another, higher force struggling with her mind and vocal cords to translate these thoughts into words so that I could understand them.

During the course of her remaining therapy sessions, Catherine relayed many more messages from the Masters. Beautiful messages about life and death, about spiritual dimensions and the purpose of our lives on the earth. My awakening had begun. My skepticism was eroding.

I remember thinking, "Since she's correct about my father and my son, could she also be correct about past lives and reincarnation, about the immortality of the soul?"

I believe so.

The Masters also spoke about past lives.

"We choose when we will come into our physical state and when we will leave. We know when we have accomplished what we were sent down here to accomplish. We know when the time is up, and you will accept your death. For you know that you can get nothing more out of this lifetime. When you have time, when you have had the time to rest and re-energize your soul, you are allowed to choose your re-entry back into the physical state. Those people who hesitate, who are not sure of their return here, they might lose the chance that was given them, a chance to fulfill what they must when they're in physical state."

Since my experience with Catherine, I have regressed more than one thousand individual patients to their past lives. Very, very few of them could reach the level of the Masters. However, I have observed amazing clinical improvement in most of these people. I have seen patients remember a name during the recall of a recent lifetime and subsequently find old records that validate the existence of that past-life person, confirming the details of the memory. Some patients have even found the graves of their own previous physical bodies.

I have observed a few patients who while in regression are able to speak portions of languages they have never learned, or have never even heard, in their current lifetime. I have also studied some children who have spontaneously exhibited this ability, which is known as xenoglossy.

I have read the findings of other scientists who are independently practicing past-life regression therapy and who are reporting results extremely similar to mine.

As described in detail in my second book, *Through Time into Healing*, this therapy can benefit many types of patients, especially those with emotional and psychosomatic disorders.

Regression therapy is also extremely useful in recognizing and stopping recurrent destructive patterns, such as drug or alcohol abuse and problems in relationships.

Many of my patients recall habits, traumas, and abusive relationships that not only occurred in their past lifetimes but are again occurring in the current life. For example, one patient remembered a violently abusive husband in a past life who has resurfaced in the present as her violent father. One warring couple discovered they had been killing each other in four previous lifetimes together. The stories and the patterns go on and on.

When the recurring pattern has been recognized, when its causes have been understood, it can be broken. There is no sense in continuing the pain.

Neither the therapist nor the patient has to believe in past lives for the technique and process of regression therapy to work. But if they try it, clinical improvement often results.

Spiritual growth almost always results.

I once regressed a man from South America who remembered a guilt-ridden lifetime as part of the team that helped to develop and ultimately drop the atomic bomb on Hiroshima in order to end World War II. Now a radiologist in a major hospital, this man uses radiation and modern technology to save lives rather than to erase them. He is a gentle, beautiful, caring man in this life.

This is an example of how a soul can evolve and be transformed even through the most ignoble of lifetimes. It is the learning that is important, not the judgment. He learned from his World War II lifetime, and he has applied the skills and knowledge to help other souls in the current lifetime. The guilt from the first lifetime is not important. It is only important to learn from the past, not to ruminate and to feel guilty about it.

According to a *USA Today*/CNN/Gallup Poll conducted on December 18, 1994, belief in reincarnation is increasing in the United States, a country that lags behind most of the rest of the world in this belief. Twenty-seven percent of adults in the United States believe in reincarnation, up from 21 percent in 1990.

There is more. The number who believe that there can be contact with the dead has risen from 18 percent in 1990 to 28 percent in December 1994. Ninety percent believe in heaven, and 79 percent believe in miracles.

I can almost hear the spirits clapping.

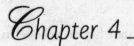

Chapter 4

So the idea of reincarnation contains a most comforting explanation of reality by means of which Indian thought surmounts difficulties which baffle the thinkers of Europe.

ALBERT SCHWEITZER

Elizabeth's first experience with regression occurred the following week. I quickly put her into a deep state of hypnosis by using a rapid-induction method in order to bypass the blocks and obstacles that the conscious mind often constructs.

Hypnosis is a state of focused concentration, but the ego, the mind, has the ability to interfere with this concentration by bringing up distracting thoughts. In using a rapid-induction technique, I was able to put Elizabeth into a deep hypnotic state within a minute.

I had given her a relaxation tape to play at home during the week between her appointments. I had recorded this tape to help my patients practice the techniques of self-hypnosis. I found that the more they practice at home, the deeper they seem to go in the office. The tape also helps patients to relax, and it often helps them to fall asleep.

Elizabeth tried listening to the tape at home, but she

couldn't relax. She felt much too anxious. What if something happened? She worried that because she was alone there was nobody to help her.

Her mind "protected" her by allowing everyday thoughts to crowd in and distract her from the tape. Between her nervousness and her thoughts, she couldn't concentrate.

As she described her experience at home with the tape, I decided to use a more rapid method of hypnosis to move her beyond the obstacles that her mind and her fears were creating.

The most common technique used to induce the hypnotic trance is called progressive relaxation. Beginning by having the patient slow her breathing, the therapist then talks the patient into a deeply relaxed state by instructing the patient to gently and sequentially relax her muscles. Then she is asked to visualize or imagine beautiful and relaxing scenes. By using techniques such as counting backward, the therapist helps the patient go even deeper.

By this time, the patient is in a light to moderate hypnotic trance, which the therapist can then deepen if desired. The whole process takes about fifteen minutes.

During this fifteen minutes, however, the patient's mind can disrupt the hypnotic process by thinking or analyzing or debating instead of relaxing and flowing with the suggestions.

Accountants and other people who have been drilled to think in a logical, linear, highly rational pattern frequently allow the chatter of their minds to disrupt the process. Even though I felt Elizabeth could go under deeply no matter which technique I used, I decided to use a more rapid method anyway, just to be sure.

I told Elizabeth to sit forward in her chair, to keep her

gaze fixed on my eyes, and to press down with her right
hand, which was palm to palm with mine. I was standing
in front of her.

As she applied the pressure to my hand, with her body
tilted slightly forward in the chair, I talked to her. Her
eyes were fixed on mine.

Suddenly and without any warning, I pulled away my
hand, which was underneath hers. Her body, now unsup-
ported, lurched forward. At this precise moment, I said
"Sleep!" very loudly.

Instantly, Elizabeth's body collapsed back into the chair.
She was already in a deep hypnotic trance. While her
conscious mind had been preoccupied with the sudden
loss of balance, my command to sleep traveled directly
and without any interference to her subconscious. She
went directly into a state of conscious "sleep," which is
the equivalent of hypnosis.

"You can remember everything, every experience you
have ever had," I told her. We could now begin the
journey backward.

I wanted to see which of her senses predominated in
her recollections so I asked her to go back to her last
pleasant meal, and I instructed her to use all of her senses
as she remembered the meal. She remembered the smell,
the taste, the sight, and the feeling of a recent dinner so
I knew she had the ability for vivid recall. It seemed, in
her case, that the visual sense was the most predominant.

And then I took her back into her childhood to see if she
could retrieve a memory from a placid period in her Minnesota childhood. She smiled a little girl's contented smile.

"I'm in the kitchen with my mother. She looks very
young. I'm young, too. I'm little. I'm about five. And
we're cooking. We're making pies . . . and cookies. It's

fun. My mother's happy. I can see it all, the apron, her hair up. I can smell the smells. They're wonderful."

"Walk into another room and tell me what you see," I instructed her.

She walked into the living room. She described the large dark wood furniture, the well-worn floors. And then a portrait of her mother, a photograph that was on a dark wooden table next to a big comfortable chair.

"I see my mother in the picture," Elizabeth went on. "She's beautiful . . . so young. I see the pearls around her neck. She loves those pearls. They're for special occasions. The beautiful white dress . . . her dark hair . . . her eyes are so bright and so healthy."

"Good," I said, "I'm glad you remember her and that you can see her so clearly."

The virtual certainty of remembering a recent meal or a childhood scene helps build the patient's confidence in his or her ability to recall memories. These memories show the patient that hypnosis works and that it is not frightening, that the process can even be pleasant. The patient sees that recalled memories are often more vivid and more detailed than the memories of the conscious, waking mind.

After emerging from the trance, patients almost always consciously remember memories recalled during hypnosis. Only rarely are patients in such a deep state that they have amnesia for what was experienced. Although I frequently tape-record regression sessions to ensure accuracy and to refer to when necessary, the tapes are more for me than for the patients. They remember vividly.

"Now we will go even further back. Don't worry what is imagination, what is fantasy, what is metaphor or symbol, actual memory or some combination of all of these," I told her. "Just let yourself experience. Try not to let your mind judge or criticize or even comment on the material you are experiencing. Just experience it. This is only for the experience. You can critique it afterward. You can analyze it later. But for now just let yourself experience.

"We're going back into the womb now, into the in-utero period, just before you were born. Whatever pops into your mind is fine. Just let yourself experience it."

And I counted back from five to one, deepening her state of hypnosis.

Elizabeth felt herself inside her mother's womb. It was warm and safe, and she could feel her mother's love. A tear trickled down from the corner of each of her closed eyes.

She remembered how much her parents had wanted her, especially her mother. The tears were tears of happiness and of nostalgia.

Elizabeth could already feel the love that would greet her birth, and this made her feel very happy.

Her experience in the womb is not positive proof that the memory is accurate, or that it is indeed a complete memory. But to Elizabeth the sensations and emotions were so strong and so powerful that they were real to her, and this made her feel much better.

While under hypnosis, a patient of mine remembered being born as a twin. The other baby was stillborn. However, the patient never knew that she had a twin sister. Her parents had never told her about her stillborn sibling. When she told her parents about her experience under hypnosis, they confirmed the complete accuracy of her recall. She was indeed a twin.

Usually, however, memories from the womb are difficult to validate.

"Are you ready to go further back now?" I asked,

hoping Elizabeth had not become frightened by the intensity of her emotions.

"Yes," she answered calmly. "I'm ready."

"Good," I said. "Now we're going back to see if you can remember anything from before birth, either in a mystical or spiritual state, in another dimension, or even in a past life. Whatever pops into your mind is fine. Don't critique it. Don't worry about it. Just experience. Let yourself experience."

I had her imagine herself walking into an elevator and pushing a button as I slowly counted backward from five to one. The elevator traveled back through time and through space, and the door opened when I said "one." I instructed her to step outside and join the figure, the scene, the experience on the other side of the door. But it was not what I expected.

"It's so dark," she said, with terror in her voice. "I've . . . I've fallen off the boat. It's so cold. It's terrible."

"If you become uncomfortable," I quickly interrupted, "just float above the scene and watch it as if you are watching a movie. But if you're not uncomfortable, stay with it. See what happens. See what you experience."

The experience was frightening to her, so she floated above. Elizabeth could see herself as a teenage boy. Having fallen off a boat in a storm at night, this boy had drowned in the dark waters. Suddenly her breathing slowed noticeably, and she seemed more peaceful. She had detached from the body.

"I have left that body," Elizabeth said, almost matter of factly.

This had all happened extremely rapidly. Before I had time to explore the lifetime, she was already out of that body. I wanted her to review what had happened, to tell me what she could see and understand.

"What were you doing on the boat?" I asked her, trying to back up in time even though she was already out of her body.

"I was traveling with my father," she said. "And a sudden storm came up. The boat began to take on water. It was very unstable and rocking wildly. The waves were huge, and I was swept over the side."

"What happened to the other people?" I asked.

"I don't know," she said. "I was swept over the side. I don't know what happened to them."

"About how old are you when this happens?"

"I don't know," she answered. "About twelve or thirteen. A young teenager."

Elizabeth did not seem eager to volunteer any more details. She had left that life early, both in that lifetime and in remembering it in my office. We could not get any more information. And so I awakened her.

The following week, Elizabeth seemed less depressed even though I had prescribed no antidepressant medication to treat her symptoms of grief and depression.

"I feel lighter," she said. "I feel freer, and I find I'm not as uncomfortable in the dark."

Elizabeth had always been somewhat uneasy in the dark, and she avoided going out alone at night. At home, she often kept all the lights on. But in the past week she had noticed improvement with this symptom. Unbeknownst to me, swimming made her feel uneasy and somewhat anxious, but in the past week she was able to spend time in the pool and jacuzzi in her condominium complex. Although these were not her main concerns, she was pleased that these symptoms were diminishing.

So many of our fears are based in the past, not the future. Often the things we fear the most have already happened either in childhood or in a past life. Because we have forgotten or only dimly remember, we fear that the traumatic event may become real in our future.

But Elizabeth was still very sad, and we had not found her mother except in a childhood memory. The search would continue.

Elizabeth's story is fascinating. Pedro's is similarly so. Yet their stories are not completely unique. Many of my patients have suffered from profound grief, from fears and phobias, from frustrating relationships. Many have found their lost loved ones in other times and other places. Many have been able to heal their grief as they remember past lifetimes and reach spiritual states.

Some of the people I have regressed are celebrities. Some are seemingly ordinary people with amazing stories. Their experiences reflect the universal themes embodied in the unfolding journeys of Elizabeth and Pedro as they approach the crossroads of destiny.

We are all walking along the same path.

In November of 1992 I traveled to New York City to regress Joan Rivers as part of a segment for her television talk show. We had arranged for the regression to be taped in a private hotel suite several days prior to the live taping of Joan's show. Joan arrived late, delayed by Howard Stern, the radio host who was her uninhibited guest on that day's show. She was not very relaxed, still in her television makeup, jewelry, and a beautiful red sweater.

As we talked prior to the regression, I learned that she was still grieving the deaths of her mother and her husband. Although her mother had died years earlier, their relationship had been very intense, and Joan continued to miss her greatly. Her husband's death was more recent.

Joan sat stiffly in a plush, beige-patterned chair. The cameras began to record an extraordinary scene.

Soon Joan slumped down into the chair, her chin resting precariously on the palm of her hand. Her breathing slowed and she went deeply into the hypnotic state. "I went under *very* deeply," she later said.

The regression began, and we went backward through time. Her first stop was at the age of four. She remembered stress at home caused by a visit from her grandmother. Joan could see herself vividly.

"I'm wearing a checked dress with Mary Jane shoes and white socks."

We left for a more distant time. The year was 1835, and she was in England, where she was a woman of the gentry.

"I have dark hair, and I'm taller and slim," she observed. She had three children.

"One is definitely my mother," she added. Joan recognized that one of her children in that lifetime, a six-year-old daughter, had reincarnated as her present-day mother.

"How do you know it's her?" I asked.

"I just *know* it's her," she responded emphatically. Soul recognition often transcends verbal description. There is an intuitive knowing, a knowledge of the heart. Joan Rivers *knew* that this little girl and her mother were the same soul.

She did not recognize the Englishwoman's husband,

who was also tall and slim, as someone in her present life. "He's wearing a beaver top hat," she elaborated. He was formally dressed. "We're walking in a large park with gardens," she noted.

Joan began to cry and wanted to leave that time. One of her children was dying.

"It's her!" she sobbed, meaning the daughter whom she recognized as her mother in her current lifetime. "Terrible . . . terribly sad!" The young girl died, and we left that time and place.

We moved even further back in time, back into the eighteenth century.

"It's seventeen [hundred] something. . . . I'm a farmer, a man." She seemed surprised at the change of gender, but this was a happier lifetime.

"I'm a very good farmer because I love the earth so much," she observed. In her current life, Joan loves to work in her gardens, where she finds peace and a respite from her hectic show-business life.

I gently awakened her. Her grief was already beginning to heal. She understood that her precious mother, who was her young daughter in 1835 England, was a soul companion across the centuries. Even though they were now once more separated, Joan knew that they would be together again, in another time and another place.

Elizabeth, who did not know about Joan's experience, came to me seeking a similar healing. Would she, too, find her beloved mother?

Meanwhile, in the same office and in the same chair, separated from Elizabeth by only the minuscule gulf of a few days, another drama was in progress.

Pedro was suffering. His life was burdened with sadness, unshared secrets, and hidden longings.

And the most important meeting of his life was silently but rapidly approaching.

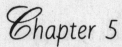

Chapter 5 _____

And still her grief would not abate.
At last she bore another child, and great
Was the father's joy; and loud his cry: "A Son!"
That day, to thus rejoice—he was the only one.
Dejected and wan the mother lay; her soul was numb. . . .
Then suddenly she cried with anguish wild,
Her thoughts less on the new than on the absent child. . . .
"My angel in his grave, and I not at his side!"
Speaking through the babe now held in her embrace
She hears again the well-known voice adored:
"Tis I,—but do not tell!" He gazes at her face.

VICTOR HUGO

*P*edro is an extraordinarily handsome Mexican man, more fair than I had anticipated, with sandy brown hair and wonderful blue eyes that at times seem almost green. His charm and easy wit hid the grief he was feeling at the death of his brother, who had died ten months previously in a terrible automobile accident in Mexico City.

Many people suffering from acute grief reactions come to see me, hoping to understand more about death or even to encounter their deceased loved ones again. The meeting might occur in a past lifetime. It might occur in the spiritual state found in-between lifetimes. Or the reunion might take place in a mystical setting, beyond the confines of the physical body and physical geography.

Whether the spiritual meetings are real or imaginary,

they possess a power that is vividly felt by the patient. Lives are changed.

The delicate and often detailed recall of past lifetimes is not a wish fulfillment. Images are not merely conjured up because a patient needs them or because they might make him feel better. What is remembered is what has happened.

The specificity and accuracy of remembered details, the depth of emotion displayed, the resolution of clinical symptoms, and the life-transforming power of the memories all point to the reality of the recall.

The unusual aspect of Pedro's story was the ten months that had elapsed since his brother's death. By this time, grief is generally resolving. The long time span of Pedro's grief suggested an underlying, even deeper despair.

His sadness actually extended far beyond his brother's death. We would learn in subsequent sessions that he had been separated from his loved ones over many lifetimes, and he was acutely sensitized to the loss of a love. The sudden death of his brother reminded him, in the deepest unconscious recesses of his mind, of losses even greater, even more tragic, over millennia.

In psychiatric theory, each loss we experience stirs repressed or forgotten feelings and memories of previous losses. Our grief is magnified by the cumulative grief of earlier losses.

In my research with past lives, I was finding that the arena in which these losses occur needs to be enlarged. We cannot go back only to childhood. Earlier, past-life losses need to be included. Some of our most tragic losses and our most profound grief happened before we were born.

Before anything, I needed to know more about Pedro's life. I needed landmarks to navigate the flow of future sessions.

"Tell me about yourself," I asked. "Your childhood, your family, and whatever else you feel is important. Tell me everything you think I should know."

Pedro sighed deeply and sank back into the large, soft chair. He loosened his tie and unbuttoned the top button of his shirt. His body language told me this would not be easy for him.

Pedro came from a very privileged family, both financially and politically. His father owned a large business and several factories. They lived in the hills above the city, in a spectacular house within a secure, gated community.

Pedro had attended the finest private schools in the city. He had studied English since the early grades, and after living in Miami for several years, his English was excellent. He was the youngest of three children. His sister was the oldest child, and even though she was four years older than he, Pedro was extremely protective of her. His brother was two years older and very close to Pedro.

Pedro's father worked very hard and usually didn't come home until late at night. His mother and the nannies, maids, and other staff ran the house and cared for the children.

Pedro studied business in college. He had several girl-friends, but no serious relationship.

"Somehow my mother was never very fond of the girls I dated," Pedro added. "She always found some particular fault and never let me forget."

At this point, Pedro looked around uncomfortably.

"What is it?" I inquired.

He didn't respond immediately, swallowing several times before beginning.

"I had an affair with an older woman during my last year at the university," he slowly told me. "She was older . . . and married." Pedro paused.

"Okay," I responded after a few moments, mostly to fill the silence. I could feel his discomfort, and despite many years of experience, I still didn't like the feeling. "Did her husband find out?"

"No," he answered, "he didn't."

"Things could have been worse," I pointed out, stating the obvious, trying to comfort him.

"There is more," he added ominously.

I nodded, waiting for Pedro to fill me in.

"She became pregnant. . . . There was an abortion. My parents don't know about this." His eyes were cast downward. He was still ashamed and feeling guilty, years after the affair and the abortion.

"I understand," I began. "Can I tell you what I have learned about abortions?" I asked him.

He nodded his assent. He knew about my research into hypnosis and past lives.

"An abortion, or a miscarriage, usually involves an agreement between the mother and the soul that would enter the baby. Either the baby's body would not be healthy enough to carry out its planned tasks in the coming life," I continued, "or the timing was not right for its purposes, or the outside situation had changed, such as the desertion of the father when the baby's or mother's plans required a father figure. Do you understand?"

"Yes," he nodded, but he didn't look convinced. I knew that his strong Catholic background might make the resolution of his guilt and shame more difficult. Sometimes our old, fixed beliefs interfere with the acquisition of new knowledge.

I went back to the basics.

"I will tell you only about my own research," I explained, "not about what I have read or heard about from others. This information comes from my patients, usually when they are deeply hypnotized. Sometimes the words are theirs, and sometimes they seem to be coming from another, higher source."

Pedro nodded his head again, not speaking.

"My patients tell me that the soul does not enter the body right away. Around the time of conception, a reservation is made by the soul. No other soul can have that body. The soul who has reserved that particular baby's body can then come into and out of the body, as it wishes. It is not confined. This is similar to people in comas," I added.

Pedro nodded in understanding, still not speaking but listening intently.

"During pregnancy, the soul is gradually more and more attached to the baby's body," I went on, "but the attachment is not complete until around the time of birth, either shortly before, during, or just afterward."

I emphasized this concept by joining my hands at the base of my palms, forming a ninety-degree angle. Then I slowly closed my hands so that the rest of my palms and my fingers met, like the universal hand symbol for prayer, denoting the gradual attachment of the soul to the body.

"You can never harm or kill a soul," I added. "The soul is immortal and indestructible. It will find a way to return, if that is the plan."

"What do you mean?" Pedro asked.

"I have had cases where the same soul, after a miscarriage or abortion, comes back to the same parents in their next baby."

"Incredible!" Pedro responded. His face appeared brighter now, not so guilty or embarrassed.

"You never know," I added.

After a few moments of contemplation, Pedro sighed again and crossed his legs, adjusting his pants. We had shifted back into the history-taking mode.

"What happened after that?" I asked.

"After graduation, I went back home. At first I worked in the factories, learning more about the business. Later on I came to Miami to run the business here and abroad. I've been here since," he explained.

"How is the business going?"

"Very well, but it occupies too much of my time."

"Is that a big problem?"

"It doesn't help my love life," Pedro said, grinning. He was not entirely joking. Now twenty-nine years old, he felt that he was racing past the time to find love, marry, and start a family. Racing, but no prospects.

"Are you having relationships with women?"

"Yes," he answered, "but nothing special. I haven't really fallen in love. . . . I hope I can," he added with some concern in his voice. "I will very soon have to return to Mexico and live there," Pedro mused, "in order to take over my brother's duties. Perhaps I will meet someone there," he commented without conviction.

I wondered if his mother's criticisms of Pedro's girlfriends and the experience of the affair and the abortion were psychological obstacles to a loving and intimate relationship. We would look at those issues later, I thought.

"And how is your family in Mexico?" I asked, lightening the mood while continuing to collect information.

"They are well. My father is more than seventy now, so my brother and I—" Pedro stopped abruptly. He swallowed and took a deep breath before resuming. "So I have more responsibility in the business," he concluded in a quiet voice.

"My mother is also well." He paused before amending his answer. "But they are both not coping well with the death. It has taken a great deal out of them. They have grown much older."

"And your sister?"

"She is sad also, but she has her husband and her children," Pedro explained.

I nodded my head in understanding. She had more distractions to help her cope.

Pedro was in excellent physical health. His only complaint was of intermittent pain in his neck and left shoulder, but this problem had been present for a very long time, and doctors had not found anything unusual.

"I've learned to live with it," Pedro told me.

I became aware of time. Looking at my watch, I saw that we had run twenty minutes late. My internal alarm clock was usually much more reliable.

I must have been really absorbed in the drama of Pedro's story, I rationalized silently, unaware that even more absorbing dramas were only now beginning to unfold.

The Vietnamese Buddhist monk and philosopher, Thich Nhat Hanh, writes about enjoying a good cup of tea. You must be completely awake in the present to enjoy the tea. Only in the awareness of the present can your hands feel the pleasant warmth of the cup. Only in the present can you savor the aroma, taste the sweetness, appreciate the delicacy. If you are ruminating about the past or worrying about the future, you will completely miss the experience of enjoying the cup of tea. You will look down at the cup, and the tea will be gone.

Life is like that. If you are not fully in the present, you will look around and it will be gone. You will have missed the feel, the aroma, the delicacy and beauty of life. It will seem to be speeding past you.

The past is finished. Learn from it and let it go. The future is not even here yet. Plan for it, but do not waste your time worrying about it. Worrying is worthless. When you stop ruminating about what has already happened, when you stop worrying about what might never happen, then you will be in the present moment. Then you will begin to experience joy in life.

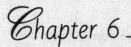

Chapter 6 _____

> I hold that when a person dies
> His Soul returns again to earth;
> Arrayed in some new flesh-disguise,
> Another mother gives him birth.
> With sturdier limbs and brighter brain
> The old soul takes the road again.
>
> JOHN MASEFIELD

*P*edro returned to the office one week later for his second appointment. Grief still tormented him, robbing him of simple pleasures and interfering with his sleep. He began by telling me about an unusual dream he had dreamt twice in the past week.

"I was dreaming about something else when all of a sudden an older woman appeared," Pedro explained.

"Did you recognize the woman?" I asked.

"No," he answered immediately. "She appeared to be in her sixties or seventies. She wore a beautiful white dress, but she was not at peace. Her face was anguished. She reached out to me, and she kept repeating the same words."

"What did she say?"

"'Hold her hand. . . . Hold her hand. You will know. Reach out to her. Hold her hand.' That is what she said."

"Hold whose hand?"

"I don't know. She just said 'Hold her hand.'"

37

"Was there anything more in the dream?"

"Not really. But I did notice that she was holding a white feather in one hand."

"What does that mean?" I asked.

"You're the doctor," Pedro reminded me.

Yes, I thought. I'm the doctor. I knew that symbols could mean almost anything, depending on the unique experiences of the dreamer as well as the universal archetypes described by Carl Jung or the popular symbols of Sigmund Freud.

This dream, somehow, did not feel Freudian.

I responded to the "You're the doctor" comment and its implied need to be answered.

"I'm not sure," I answered truthfully. "It could mean a lot of things. The white feather could symbolize peace or a spiritual state or many other things. We will have to explore the dream," I added, relegating its interpretation to the future.

"I had the dream again last night," Pedro said.

"Same woman?"

"Same woman, same words, same feather," Pedro clarified. " 'Hold her hand. . . . Hold her hand. Reach out to her. Hold her hand.' "

"Perhaps the answers will come during the regressions," I suggested. "Are you ready?"

He nodded, and we began. I already knew that Pedro could reach a deep level of hypnosis because I had checked his eyes.

The ability to roll the eyes upward, trying to look at the top of the head, and then to allow the eyelids to slowly flutter down while keeping the eyes gazing upward is highly correlated with the ability to be deeply hypnotized.

I measure how much of the sclera, or white part of the eye, is showing when the eye reaches its apex. I also observe how much white is showing while the eyelids slowly close. The more white showing, the deeper the person can go.

Pedro's eyes had nearly disappeared into his head when I tested him. Only the tiniest part of the bottom rim of his iris, the colored part of the eye, remained. As his eyelids fluttered closed, the iris did not descend at all. He could reach a deep trance state.

I was mildly surprised, then, when Pedro found it difficult to relax. Since the eye-roll test measured the physical ability to relax deeply and to reach profound levels of hypnosis, I knew his mind was interfering. Sometimes patients who are used to being in control have some initial reluctance to just let go.

"Just relax," I advised him. "Don't worry about what comes into your mind. It doesn't matter if you experience anything today or not. This is practice," I added, trying to remove any pressure he was feeling. I knew he desperately wanted to find his brother.

As I talked, Pedro relaxed more and more. He began to enter a deeper level. His breathing slowed, and his muscles softened. He appeared to sink even deeper into the white leather recliner. His eyes moved slowly under his closed eyelids as he began to visualize images.

I took him slowly back in time.

"At first, just go back and remember the last pleasant meal that you have eaten. Use all of your senses. Remember completely. See who was there with you. Remember your feelings," I instructed.

He did this, but he remembered several meals, not just one. He was still trying to maintain control.

"Relax even deeper," I urged. "Hypnosis is only a form of focused concentration. You never give up control. You are always in charge. All hypnosis is self-hypnosis."

His breathing deepened even more.

"You are always in control," I told him. "If you ever get anxious while having a memory or experience, you can just float above it and watch from a distance, like watching a movie. Or you can leave the scene entirely and go anywhere you want, visualize the beach, or your house, or any other safe place for you. If you're very uncomfortable, you can even open your eyes and you'll be awake and alert back here, if you wish.

"This is not *Star Trek*," I added. "You don't get beamed anywhere. These are only memories, like any other memories, just like you remembered the pleasant meals. You are always in control."

Now he let go. I took him back to his childhood and Pedro smiled broadly.

"I can see the dogs and horses on the farm," he told me. His family owned a farm a few hours outside the city, and many happy weekends and vacations were spent there.

The family was together. His brother was alive, vibrant, laughing. I remained silent for a few moments, letting Pedro enjoy more of this childhood memory.

"Are you ready to go even further back?" I asked.

"Yes."

"Good. Let us see if you can remember anything from a past life." I counted backward from five to one as Pedro visualized himself walking through a magnificent door into another time and another place, into a past lifetime.

As soon as I reached the number one, I saw his eyes

fluttering wildly. He was instantly alarmed. He started to sob.

"It's terrible . . . terrible!" He gasped. "They're all killed. . . . They're all dead." The remains of bodies were strewn everywhere. Fire had destroyed the village, with its odd rounded tents. Only one tent remained intact, standing incongruously on the periphery of the carnage and destruction. Its colored flags and large white feathers fluttered wildly in the cold sunlight.

The horses, the cattle, and the oxen were gone. It was apparent that nobody had survived this massacre. The "cowards" from the east had done this.

"No wall, no warlords will protect them from me," Pedro vowed. Revenge would have to come later. He was numbed, hopeless, devastated.

I have learned over the years that people in their first regression often gravitate to the most traumatic event in a lifetime. This occurs because the emotion of the trauma is so strongly impressed upon their psyches and carried by the soul into future incarnations.

I wanted to know more. What preceded this horrific experience? What happened afterward?

"Go back in time within that lifetime," I urged. "Go back to happier times. What do you remember?"

"There are many yurts . . . tents. We are a powerful people," he answered. "I am happy here." Pedro described a nomadic people who hunted and raised cattle. His parents were leaders, and he was a strong and skilled horseman and hunter.

"The horses are very swift. They are small with large tails," he said.

He married the most beautiful girl of his people, one

with whom he had played as a child and whom he had loved as long as he could remember. He could have married the daughter of a neighboring chief, but he married for love.

"What is the name of this land?" I asked.

He hesitated. "I think you call it Mongolia."

I knew that Mongolia probably had a very different name when Pedro was there. The language was completely different. So how could Pedro, speaking from that time, know the word *Mongolia*? Because he was remembering, his memories were being filtered through his present-day mind.

The process is similar to watching a movie. The present-day mind is very much aware, watching and commenting. The mind compares the movie's characters and themes with those of the current life. The patient is the movie's observer, its critic, and its star, all at the same time. The patient is able to use his present-day knowledge of history and geography to help date and locate places and events. Throughout the movie he can remain in the deeply hypnotized state.

Pedro could vividly remember the Mongolia that existed many centuries ago, yet he could speak English and answer my questions while remembering.

"Do you know your name?"

Again, he hesitated. "No, it does not come to me."

There was little else. He had a child, and the birth was a great happiness not only to Pedro and his wife but also to his parents and the rest of the people. His wife's parents had both died several years before the marriage, so she was not only a wife to him but also a daughter to his parents.

Pedro was exhausted. He did not want to return to the devastated village to once again confront the remains of his shattered life so I awakened him.

When a memory from a past life is traumatic and overflowing with emotion, it can be very useful to go back a second time, and perhaps a third. At each repetition the negative emotion is lessened and the patient remembers even more. He also learns more, as the emotional blocks and distractions are diminished. I knew Pedro had more to learn from this ancient life.

Pedro was giving himself another two or three months to resolve his personal and business affairs in Miami. We still had plenty of time to explore the Mongolian lifetime in more detail. We had time to explore other lifetimes as well. We had not yet found his brother. Instead he had found another devastating series of losses: beloved wife, child, parents, community.

Was I helping him or was I adding even more to his burden? Only time would tell.

After one of my workshops, a participant told me a marvelous story.

From the time she was a little girl, if she let her hand hang over the side of her bed, another hand would lovingly take hers, and she would be reassured no matter how anxious she was feeling. Oftentimes when her hand accidentally went over the bedside and the grasp surprised her, she would reflexively jerk back her hand, and this always broke the embrace.

She always knew when to reach for the hand and to feel comforted. There was, of course, no physical form under her bed.

As she grew older, the hand remained. She married but never told her husband about this experience because it seemed so childlike.

When she became pregnant with her first child, the hand disappeared. She missed her loving and familiar companion. There was no hand to take hers in that same loving way.

Her baby was born, a beautiful daughter. A little while after the birth, while lying in bed together, the baby took her hand. A sudden and powerful recognition of that old familiar feeling flooded her mind and her body.

Her protector had returned. She cried with happiness and felt a great surge of love and a connection that she knew existed far beyond the physical.

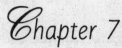

Chapter 7

> *Wert thou that just Maid who once before*
> *Forsook the hated earth, O tell me sooth,*
> *And cam'st again to visit us once more?*
> *Or wert thou that sweet smiling Youth? . . .*
> *Or any other of that heavenly brood*
> *Let down in cloudy throne to do the world good?*
> *Or wert thou of the golden-winged host,*
> *Who, having clad thyself in human weed,*
> *To earth from thy prefixed seat didst post*
> *And after short abode fly back with speed*
> *As if to show what creatures heaven doth breed;*
> *Thereby to set the hearts of men on fire,*
> *To scorn the sordid world, and unto Heaven aspire?*
>
> JOHN MILTON

Elizabeth seemed less depressed as she entered my office for her third appointment. Her eyes were brighter.

"I feel lighter," she told me. "I feel freer. . . ." Her brief recollection of herself as the young boy swept off the boat had begun to sweep away some of her fears. Not just the fears of water or of the dark, but also deeper and more basic fears, fears of death and extinction.

She had died as that boy, and yet here she was again, as Elizabeth. At a subconscious level, her grief might have been lessening because of the knowledge that she had lived before and would live again, that death was not final.

45

And if she could spring back again, renewed and refreshed, in a new body, then so could her loved ones. So can we all, reborn to deal once more with the joys and hardships, with the triumphs and tragedies of life on earth.

Elizabeth quickly went into a deep hypnotic trance. Within a few minutes, her eyes were sweeping from side to side under her closed lids as she scanned an ancient vista.

"The sand is beautiful," she began, recalling a life as a Native American in the South, probably on the west coast of Florida. "It's so white . . . almost pink at times. . . . It's so fine, like sugar." She paused for a moment. "The sun sets over the big sea. To the east are large swamps, with many birds and animals. There are lots of small islands between the swamps and the sea. The waters are filled with good fish. We catch the fish, in the rivers and between the islands." She paused again, then continued.

"We are at peace. My life is very happy. My family is large; I seem to be related to many in the village. I know about roots, plants, and herbs. . . . I can make medicines from plants. . . . I know about healing."

In Native American cultures there was no penalty for using healing potions or for other holistic practices. Instead of being called witches and drowned or burned at the stake, healers were respected and often revered.

I took her forward in that lifetime, but no traumas emerged. Her life was peaceful and satisfying. She died of old age, surrounded by the entire village.

"There is very little sadness with my death," she noted after floating above her withered old body and surveying the scene below, "even though all of my village seem to be there."

She was not at all upset by the lack of grieving. There was great respect and caring for her, for her body and her soul. Only the sadness was missing.

"We do not mourn deaths because we know that the spirit is eternal. It returns in human form again if its work is not finished," she explained. "Sometimes by carefully examining the new body, the identity of the previous body can be known." She pondered this concept for a few moments. "We look for birthmarks where scars used to be and for other signs," she elaborated.

"Similarly, we do not celebrate births so much . . . even though it may be good to see the spirit again." She paused, perhaps searching for the words to describe this concept.

"Although the earth is very beautiful and continually demonstrates the harmony and interconnectedness of all things . . . which is a great lesson . . . life is much harder here. With the greater spirit there is no disease, no pain, no separation. . . . There is no ambition, no competition, no hatred, no fear, no enemy. . . . There is only peace and harmony. So the smaller spirit, returning, cannot be happy to leave such a place. It would be wrong for us to celebrate when the spirit is saddened. It would be very selfish and unfeeling," she concluded.

"This does not mean that we do not welcome the returning spirit," she quickly added. "It is important to demonstrate our love and affection at this vulnerable time."

Having explained this fascinating concept of death without sadness and birth without celebration, she was silent, resting.

Here again was the concept of reincarnation and the reunion in physical form of past-life family, friends, and lovers. In all times and in diverse cultures throughout history, this concept has appeared seemingly independently.

The dim memory of that ancient life might have helped to pull her back again to Florida, reminding her at the deepest levels of an ancestral home. Perhaps the feeling of sand and sea, of palms and of mangrove swamps called to her soul memory, helping to lure her back with a subconscious seduction. For that life had been most pleasant and filled with satisfactions not present in her current life.

These ancient stirrings might have led her to apply to the University of Miami, which led to her scholarship and her move to Miami. This is not coincidence. Destiny required her to be here.

"Are you tired?" I asked, returning my attention to Elizabeth, who was still resting peacefully on the recliner.

"No," she answered quietly.

"Do you want to explore another lifetime?"

"Yes." More quiet.

Once again we traveled back through time, and once again she emerged in an ancient land.

"This is a desolate land," Elizabeth observed after she had scanned the scene. "There are high mountains . . . dusty dirt roads . . . the traders pass on these roads. . . . This is a route for traders going east and west. . . ."

"Do you know the country?" I asked, looking for details.

I did not like to intrude with too many questions for the logical, or left-brain, part of the mind. Such questions could interfere with the immediacy of the experience, which is more a right-brain, or intuitive, function. But

Elizabeth was in a profoundly deep state. She could answer the questions and yet continue to vividly experience this scene. Details were important, too.

"India . . . I think," she answered hesitantly. "Maybe just west of that . . . I don't think the borders are that clear. We live in the mountains, and there are passes the traders must go through," she added, returning to the scene.

"Do you see yourself?" I asked.

"Yes . . . I'm a girl . . . about fifteen. My skin is darker, and I have black hair. My clothes are dirty. I work in the stables . . . tending to the horses and mules. . . . We are very poor. The weather is so cold; my hands are *so* cold working here." Her face grimacing, Elizabeth made fists with both hands.

This young girl was innately bright but uneducated. Life was grindingly difficult. Traders frequently abused her, sometimes leaving a little money. Her family was unable to protect her. Numbing cold and constant hunger plagued her life. There was only one bright spot in that young girl's life.

"There's a young trader who comes by often with his father and the others. He loves me, and I love him. He is funny and gentle, and we laugh a lot together. I wish he could just stay so we can be together all the time."

This was not to be. She died at the age of sixteen. Her body, already worn out because of the bitter life and elements, quickly succumbed to pneumonia. Her family was around her when she died.

As we reviewed this brief life, Elizabeth was not sad. She had learned an important lesson.

"Love is the strongest force in the world," she said

softly. "Love can grow and bloom even in frozen soil and in the harshest conditions. It exists *everywhere*, and all the time. Love is a flower for all the seasons."

Her face was filled with a beautiful smile.

A patient of mine, a Catholic attorney, had just finished recalling a European lifetime in the late Middle Ages. He had remembered his death in that lifetime, a lifetime filled with greed, violence, and deceit. He was cognizant that some of these traits had persisted into his current life.

Now, reclining in the soft leather chair in my office, he was aware of floating out of his body in that medieval lifetime. Suddenly he found himself standing in a hell-like environment, amidst fires and devils. This surprised me. Although I had encountered thousands of past-life deaths in my patients, no one had ever had an experience with hell. Almost invariably people find themselves drawn to an indescribably beautiful light, a light that renews and reenergizes the spirit. But hell?

I waited for something to happen, but he reported that nobody paid any attention to him. He was waiting, too. Minutes passed. Finally a spiritual figure, whom he identified as Jesus, appeared and walked over to him. This was the first being who even noticed him.

"Don't you realize that this is all illusion?" Jesus said to him. "Only love is real!"

And then the fires and the devils instantly disappeared, revealing the beautiful light that had been there, unseen, behind the illusion.

Sometimes you get what you expect, but it may not be real.

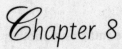

Chapter 8

*It is the secret of the world that all things subsist and
do not die, but only retire a little from sight and
afterwards return again. Nothing is dead; men feign
themselves dead, and endure mock funerals and
mournful obituaries, and there they stand looking out
of the window, sound and well, in some new strange
disguise.*

RALPH WALDO EMERSON

*B*oth Pedro and I needed to learn more about the sources
of his underlying despair, which had been deepened even
more by his brother's tragic death. We needed to understand more about the superficiality of his relationships.
Were his mother's constant criticisms of his girlfriends
and the guilt of the abortion blocking his love? Or had
he just not yet met the right woman?

The regression process is like drilling for oil. You never
quite know where the oil is, but the deeper you go the
better your chance of striking it.

Today we were going deeper.

Pedro had only recently begun to remember his past
lives. Frequently in the beginning, lifetimes are entered
at their most traumatic points. This happened again.

"I'm a soldier . . . English, I think," Pedro observed.
"Many of us are brought in by ship to capture the enemy's
fortress. It's huge, with high and very deep walls. They've

filled the harbor with large rocks. We must find another way in." He became silent as the invasion was delayed.

"Go ahead in time," I suggested. "See what happens next." I tapped him three times on his forehead in order to focus his attention and help him bridge the gap in time.

"We have overcome the rocks, and we have breached the fort," he answered. He began to grunt and to sweat. "Little tunnels . . . we are running through them, but we don't know where we are going. . . . The tunnels are narrow and low. We must go single file and bend over as we run."

Pedro began to sweat profusely. He was breathing very rapidly, and he seemed extremely upset.

"I see a tiny doorway ahead. . . . We are running through this door.

"Ugh!" he winced suddenly. "The Spanish are on the other side of the door. They're killing us as we come through, one at a time. . . . They have stuck me with a sword!" He gasped, holding his neck. His breathing became even more rapid. He was now gasping for air, and sweat was pouring from his face, drenching his shirt.

Suddenly his movements ceased. His breathing became regular, and he was calm. As I dried his forehead and face with a tissue, the sweating began to diminish.

"I'm floating above my body," Pedro announced. "I have left that life . . . so many bodies . . . so much blood below . . . but I'm above that now." He floated in silence for a few moments.

"Review that lifetime," I instructed. "What did you learn? What were the lessons?"

He pondered these questions from a higher perspective.

"I learned that violence is a profound ignorance. I died

senselessly far away from my home and loved ones. I died because of the greed of others. The English and the Spanish were both stupid, killing each other for gold in faraway lands. Stealing gold from the others and killing themselves for it. Greed and violence killed these people. . . . They had all forgotten about love."

He grew silent again. I decided to let him rest and digest these incredible lessons. I, too, began to contemplate Pedro's lessons. Over the centuries since Pedro's senseless death in a fortress far removed from his English home, gold has changed to dollars and pounds and yen and pesos, but we are still killing each other for it. Indeed, this has been going on throughout history. How very little we have learned over the centuries. How much more do we need to suffer before we once again remember about love?

Pedro's head began moving from side to side on the chair. He had an amused smile on his face. He had spontaneously entered another, much more recent lifetime. Once Pedro began to remember lifetimes, his visual experiences were particularly vivid.

"What are you experiencing?" I asked.

"I'm a woman," he observed. "I'm quite beautiful. My hair is long and blonde . . . my skin is very pale." With large blue eyes and elegant clothes, Pedro was a prostitute much in demand in post–World War I Germany. Although the country was besieged by runaway inflation, the rich still had money for her services.

Pedro had some difficulty remembering the name of this elegant woman. "Magda, I believe," he uttered. I did not want to distract him from his visual appraisal.

"I'm very successful in this business," Magda said proudly. "I'm a confidante to politicians, military leaders, and very important businessmen." She seemed a bit vain as she remembered even more.

"They are all obsessed with my beauty and my skill," she added. "I always know just what to do." Magda possessed an excellent singing voice and often performed at elegant soirees. She learned to manipulate men.

Probably from all her lifetimes as a man, I thought but did not say.

Then Pedro's voice lowered to a whisper. "I influence these people. . . . I can get them to change decisions. . . . They do it for me," she said, impressed with her status and ability to influence these powerful men.

"I usually know more than they do," she went on somewhat ruefully. "I teach *them* about politics!" Magda enjoyed power and political intrigue. Her political power, however, was indirect; it always had to be mediated through men, and this frustrated her. In a future life, Pedro would need no intermediaries.

One young man in particular stood apart from the rest.

"He is more intelligent and serious than the others," Magda observed. "His hair is brown, and his eyes are very blue. . . . He is passionate in everything he does! We spend many hours just talking. I believe we love each other, too." She did not recognize this man as anyone in her current life.

Pedro looked sad, and a tear formed in the corner of his left eye.

"I left him for another . . . an older, more powerful and wealthy man who wanted me exclusively. . . . I didn't follow my heart. I made a *terrible* mistake. He was terribly hurt by my action. He never forgave me. . . . He didn't understand." Magda had sought security and external power, putting these qualities ahead of love, the real source of security and strength.

Apparently her decision was one of those that mark a turning point in life, a fork in the road that, once chosen, cannot be undone.

Her older lover lost his power as German politics swung wildly to the violent new parties, and he abandoned her. Magda lost track of her passionate younger lover. And finally her body began to deteriorate from a chronic sexual illness, probably syphilis. She was depressed and did not have the will to resist the rampaging disease.

"Go to the end of that life," I urged her. "See what happens to you, see who is around."

"I'm in a cheap bed . . . in a hospital. This is a hospital for the poor. There are many others there, sick and moaning . . . the poorest of the poor. This must be a scene from hell!"

"Do you see yourself?

"My body is grotesque," Magda answered.

"Are there doctors and nurses around?"

"They are there," she answered bitterly. "They pay no attention to me. . . . They are not sad at all. They disapprove of my life and what I have done. They are punishing me."

A life of beauty, power, and intrigue had ended on this low note. She floated above her body, finally free.

"I feel so peaceful now," she added. "I just want to rest."

Pedro was silent in the chair. We would review that lifetime's lessons another time. He was exhausted, and I awakened him.

The chronic pain in Pedro's neck and left shoulder

gradually disappeared over the next few weeks. His physicians had never found the origins of this pain. Of course they had never considered a mortal sword wound from several centuries ago as the likely cause.

I am constantly amazed by the short-sightedness of most people. I have many acquaintances who obsess daily about their children's educations: which nursery school is the best, private schools versus public schools, which college-board prep courses are the most effective, how to maximize grades and extracurricular activities to give their children an edge to get into *that* college, *that* grad school, ad infinitum. Then the same cycle will start with their grandchildren.

But these people think that this world is frozen in time, that the future will be a replica of the present.

If we continue to chop down our forests and destroy oxygen sources, what will these children breathe in twenty or thirty years? If we poison our water systems and food cycles, what will they eat? If we blindly continue to overproduce fluorocarbons and other organic wastes and blow holes in the ozone layer, will they be able to live outdoors? If we overheat this planet by some greenhouse effect and the oceans rise and we flood our coasts and overstress oceanic and continental fault lines, where will they live? And the children and grandchildren in China and Africa and Australia and everywhere else are just as vulnerable because they are all inescapably residents of this planet. And consider this. If and when you reincarnate, you will be one of these children.

So how can we worry so much about SAT tests and colleges when there may not be a world here for our progeny?

Why is everybody so obsessed with living longer? Why squeeze a few more unhappy years out of the geriatric end? Why the preoccupation with cholesterol levels, bran diets, lipid counts, aerobic exercise, and so on?

Doesn't it make more sense to live joyously now, to make every day full, to love and be loved, rather than worry so much about your physical health in an unknown future? What if there is no future? What if death is a release into bliss?

I am not saying to neglect your body, that it is all right to smoke or to drink excessively or to abuse substances or to be grossly obese. These conditions cause pain, grief, and disability. Just don't worry so much about the future. Find your bliss today.

The irony is that, given this attitude and living happily in the present, you probably will live longer anyway.

Our bodies and our souls are like cars and their drivers. Always remember that you are the driver, not the car. Don't identify with the vehicle. The emphasis these days on prolonging the duration of our lives, on living to one hundred years of age or more, is madness. It's like keeping your old Ford going past 200,000 miles, past 300,000. The body of the car is rusting out, the transmission has been rebuilt five times, things are falling off the engine, and yet you refuse to turn it in. Meanwhile there is a brand new Corvette waiting for you right around the corner. All you have to do is gently step out of the old Ford and slide into the beautiful Corvette. The driver, the soul, never changes. Only the car.

And, by the way, I think there might be a Ferrari down the road for you.

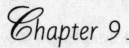

Chapter 9

*As far back as I can remember I have unconsciously
referred to the experiences of a previous state of existence. . . . I have lived in Judea eighteen hundred
years ago, but I never knew that there was such a
one as Christ among my contemporaries. As the stars
looked to me when I was a shepherd in Assyria, they
look to me now a New-Englander.*

HENRY DAVID THOREAU

$\mathscr{T}$wo weeks had elapsed between Elizabeth's appointments because she had to be away on another business
trip. Out-of-town trips were not rare for her. The beautiful smile with which she ended her last session had faded;
the realities and pressures of everyday life had once again
taken their toll.

Yet she was eager to continue the journey back through
time. She had begun to recall important events and lessons
from other lifetimes. She had experienced a glimmer of
happiness and of hope. She wanted more.

She rapidly reached a deep trance state.

Elizabeth remembered the stones of Jerusalem with
their distinctive coloring, which would change according
to the light of the day and night. At times golden. At
other times a tinge of pink or beige. But the golden color
would always return. She remembered her town near
Jerusalem with the small dirt and rock roads, the houses,
the inhabitants, their clothing, their customs. There were

some vineyards and some fig trees, some fields where flax and wheat grew. Water came from the well down the road. Ancient oaks and pomegranate trees were near the well. This was a time in Palestine, as it always seemed to be, of intense religious and spiritual activity, of new changes, always the hope and yet the heaviness, the harshness of the days, of eking out a living, of being oppressed by the invaders from Rome.

She remembered her father, named Eli, who worked at home as a potter. Using water from the well, he created shapes from clay, making bowls, jars, and many other items for his home and for the villagers, and even some to sell in Jerusalem. Sometimes merchants or others would come through the village and buy his jugs or cookware or bowls. Elizabeth supplied many more descriptions of the potter's wheel, the rhythm of her father's foot on the wheel, and details of life in this small village. Her name was Miriam, and she was a happy girl living in turbulent times. Soon her life would be forever changed by the spread of that turbulence to her village.

We progressed to the next significant event in that lifetime: her father's premature death at the hands of Roman soldiers. The Roman soldiers frequently tormented the early Christians who lived in Palestine at that time. They devised cruel games merely for their own amusement. One of these games accidentally killed Miriam's beloved father.

At first the soldiers tied Eli around the ankles and dragged him behind a horse ridden by a soldier. After an endless minute, the horse was stopped. Her father's body was battered, but he had survived the ordeal. His terrified daughter could hear the soldiers howling with laughter. They were not done with him.

Two of the Romans then wrapped the free end of the rope around their chests and began prancing around, as if they were horses. Her father lurched forward, his head striking a large rock. He was mortally injured.

The soldiers left him in the dusty road.

The senselessness of it all added to her piercing anguish, added a bitter anger and hopelessness to her father's violent demise. This was just sport to the soldiers. They had not even known her father. They had not felt his gentle touch as he tended to her minor childhood cuts and bruises. They had not heard his humor as he worked over the wheel. They had not smelled his hair after he bathed. They had not tasted his kisses or felt his hugs. They had not spent every day of their lives with this gentle, caring man.

Yet in a few terror-filled minutes they had snuffed out a beautiful life and had filled Miriam's remaining years with a grief that would never quite heal, with a loss that would never be replaced, with a hole that could never be mended. For sport. The senselessness outraged her, and tears of hatred joined those of her pain.

She rocked back and forth on the dusty blood-stained ground, her father's large head cradled in her lap. He could no longer speak. Blood trickled from the corner of his mouth. She could hear gurgling in his chest every time he labored to breathe. Death was very close. The light in his eyes approached dusk, the end of his day.

"I love you, father," she softly whispered to him, looking sadly into his darkening eyes. "I will always love you."

His dimming eyes looked back and blinked in understanding as they closed for the last time.

She kept rocking as the setting sun ended its day. Her family and the other villagers gently took his body from her so that it could be prepared. In her mind she could still see his eyes. She was sure he understood.

As I sat quietly, immobilized by the depth of Elizabeth's despair, I noticed the tape recorder was not running. I put in a new tape, and the red recording light flashed. We were recording again.

My mind connected Elizabeth's current grief to the grief from Palestine nearly two thousand years ago. Was this another case in which ancient grief was compounding current grief? Would the experience of reincarnation and knowing that there is life after death heal this grief?

I returned my attention to Elizabeth.

"Move ahead in time. Go ahead to the next significant event in that life," I instructed.

"There is none," she answered.

"What do you mean?"

"Nothing else happens of significance. I can look ahead . . . but nothing happens."

"Nothing at all?"

"No, nothing," she repeated patiently.

"Do you marry?"

"No, I don't live very long. I don't care about living. I don't really take care of myself."

Her father's death had affected her deeply, apparently leading to a profound depression and an early death.

"I have left her body," Elizabeth announced.

"What are you experiencing now?"

"I'm floating. . . . I'm floating. . . ." Her voice trailed away.

Soon she began to speak again, but the words were not hers. Her voice was deeper and very strong. Elizabeth could do what Catherine and very few of my other patients could do. She could transmit messages and information from the Masters, high-level, nonphysical beings. My first book is filled with their wisdom.

I could perceive similar messages when I meditated, but the words always seemed to be more meaningful when they came from my patients. I knew that I had to develop confidence in my own abilities to hear, to receive, and to perceive these same concepts from these same sources.

"Remember," the voice said. "Remember that you are always loved. You are always protected, and you are never alone. . . . You also are a being of light, of wisdom, of love. And you can never be forgotten. You can never be overlooked or ignored. You are not your body; you are not your brain, not even your mind. You are spirit. All you have to do is to reawaken to the memory, to remember. Spirit has no limits, not the limit of the physical body nor of the reaches of the intellect or the mind.

"As the vibrational energy of spirit is slowed down so that more dense environments such as your three-dimensional plane can be experienced, the effect is for spirit to be crystallized and transformed into denser and denser bodies. The densest of all is the physical state. The vibrational rate is the slowest. Time appears faster in this state because it is inversely related to the vibrational rate. As the vibrational rate is increased, time slows down. This is how there can be difficulty in choosing the right body, the right time of re-entry into the physical state. Because of the disparity of time, the opportunity might be missed. . . . There are many levels of consciousness, many vibrational states. It is not important that you know all of these levels.

"The first level of the seven is that which is most important to you. It is important to experience in the first plane rather than to abstract and intellectualize about the higher planes. Eventually you will have to experience them all. . . . Your task is to teach of experience—To take that which is belief and faith and transform it into experience so that the learning is complete, because experience transcends belief. Teach them to experience. Remove their fear. Teach them to love and to help one another. . . . This involves the free will of others. But to reach out with love, to reach out with compassion, to help others—this is what you must do on your plane.

"Humans always think of themselves as the only beings. This is not the case. There are many worlds and many dimensions . . . many, many more souls than there are physical containers. Also, the soul may split if it wishes and have more than one experience at the same time. This is possible but requires a level of development which most have not achieved. Eventually they will see that like a pyramid there is only one soul. And all experience is shared simultaneously. But this is not for now.

"When you look into the eyes of another, any other, and you see your own soul looking back at you, then you will know that you have reached another level of consciousness. In this sense reincarnation does not exist, for all lives and all experiences are simultaneous. But, in the three-dimensional world, reincarnation is as real as time or as a mountain or as the oceans. It is an energy like other energies, and its reality depends on the energy of the perceiver. As long as the perceiver perceives a physical body and solid objects, reincarnation is real to that perceiver. The energy consists of light and love and knowledge. The application of this knowledge in a loving way is wisdom. . . . There is currently a great lack of wisdom on your plane."

Elizabeth stopped speaking. Like Catherine, she could remember the details of her physical lifetimes but nothing of the messages she delivered from the in-between-life-times state. Both were in much deeper levels when transmitting these messages. Very few patients go so deep that amnesia is induced. Like Catherine, Elizabeth's messages could help to correct the "lack of wisdom" on our plane.

We would harvest much more knowledge before Elizabeth was through.

My contact with the wisdom of the Masters has been limited since Catherine was cured and her therapy ended. Yet in an occasional, unbelievably vivid, nearly lucid dream I will receive more information, such as the lectures near the end of *Many Lives, Many Masters*. And sometimes the messages come when I am in a deeply meditative dreamlike state. For example, a system of psychotherapy for the twenty-first century was laid out for me, a system that is psycho-spiritual in nature and which could supplant the tired techniques of the past.

The messages and images crowded my brain at great speed with a flitting, brilliant clarity. Unfortunately I could not tape-record my mind, the receiving station. So the ideas are like precious stones, but the setting—my words trying to explain and define the speeding, darting thoughts—is like dross. The beginning was a clear message.

"All is love. . . . All is love. With love comes understanding. With understanding comes patience. And then time stops. And everything is now."

Instantly I comprehended the truth of these thoughts. Reality is the present. Dwelling in the past or future causes pain and illness. Patience can stop time. God's love is everything.

I could also immediately comprehend the healing power of these thoughts. I began to understand.

"Love is the ultimate answer. Love is not an abstraction but an actual energy, or spectrum of energies, which you can 'create' and maintain in your being. Just be loving. You are beginning to touch God within yourself. Feel loving. Express your love.

"Love dissolves fear. You cannot be afraid when you are feeling love. Since everything is energy, and love encompasses all energies, all is love. This is a strong clue to the nature of God.

"When you are loving and unafraid, you can forgive. You can forgive others, and you can forgive yourself. You begin to see with the proper perspective. Guilt and anger are reflections of the same fear. Guilt is a subtle anger directed inward. Forgiveness dissolves guilt and anger. They are unnecessary, damaging emotions. Forgive. This is an act of love.

"Pride can get in the way of forgiving. Pride is one manifestation of ego. Ego is the transient, false self. You are not your body. You are not your brain. You are not your ego. You are greater than all of these. You need your ego to survive in the three-dimensional world, but you need only that part of the ego which processes information. The rest—pride, arrogance, defensiveness, fear—is worse than useless. The rest of the ego separates you from wisdom, joy, and God. You must transcend your ego and find your true self. The true self is the permanent, deepest part of you. It is wise, loving, safe, and joyful.

"Intellect is important in the three-dimensional world, but intuition is more important.

"You have reversed reality and illusion. Reality is the recognition of your immortality, divinity, and timelessness. Illusion is your transient three-dimensional world. This reversal is damaging to you. You yearn for the illusion of security instead of the security of wisdom and love. You yearn to be accepted when, in reality, you can never be rejected. Ego creates illusion and hides truth. Ego must be dissolved, then truth can be seen.

"With love and understanding comes the perspective of infinite patience. What is your hurry? There is no time anyway; it only feels that way to you. When you are not experiencing the present, when you are absorbed in the past or worried about the future, you bring great heartache and grief to yourself. Time is an illusion, too. Even in the three-dimensional world, future is only a system of probabilities. Why do you worry so?

"Therapy can be done to the self. Understanding is therapy. Love is the ultimate therapy. Therapists, teachers, and gurus can help, but only for a limited time. The direction is inward, and sooner or later the inward path must be trod alone. Although in reality you are never alone.

"Measure time, if you must, in lessons learned, not in minutes or hours or years. You can cure yourself in five minutes if you come to the proper understanding. Or in fifty years. It is all the same thing.

"The past must be remembered and then forgotten. Let it go. This is true for childhood traumas and past-life traumas. But this is also true for attitudes, misconceptions, belief systems drummed into you, for all old thoughts. Indeed, for all thoughts. How can you see freshly and clearly with all those thoughts? What if you needed to learn something new? With a fresh perspective?

"Thoughts create the illusion of separateness and difference. Ego perpetuates this illusion, and this illusion creates fear, anxiety, and tremendous grief. Fear, anxiety, and grief in turn create anger and violence. How can peace exist in the world when these chaotic emotions predominate? Just unravel. Go back to the source of the problem. You are back to thoughts, old thoughts. Stop thinking. Instead, use your intuitive wisdom to experience love again. Meditate. See that everything is interconnected and interdependent. See the unity, not the differences. See your true self. See God.

"Meditation and visualization will help you stop thinking so much and will help you begin the journey back. Healing will occur. You will begin to use your unused mind. You will see. You will understand. And you will grow wise. Then there will be peace.

"You have a relationship with yourself as well as with others. And you have lived in many bodies and in many times. So ask your present self why it is so fearful. Why are you afraid to take reasonable risks? Are you afraid of your reputation, afraid of what others think? These fears are conditioned from childhood or before.

"Ask yourself these questions: What's to lose? What is the worst that can happen? Am I content to live the rest of my life this way? Against a background of death, is this so risky?

"In your growth, do not be afraid of evoking anger in other people. Anger is only a manifestation of their insecurity. But fearing this anger can hold you back. Anger would be merely stupid if it didn't create so much grief. Dissolve your own anger in love and forgiveness.

"Do not let depression or anxiety hold you back in your growth. Depression is losing perspective, forgetting, and taking things for granted. Sharpen your focus. Reset your values. *Remember* what should not be taken for granted. Shift your perspective, and remember what is important and what is less important. Get out of the rut. Remember to hope.

"Anxiety is being lost in the ego. It is losing one's boundaries. There is a dimly remembered loss of love, a wounding of pride, a loss of patience and peace. Remember, you are never alone.

"Never lose the courage to take risks. You are immortal. You can never be hurt."

Sometimes the messages are much less psychological and seem to be from an older, more didactic source. The style is quite different. It is almost as if I am taking dictation.

"There are many types of karma, debts to be balanced. Individual karma pertains to the entity's own obligations, those unique to him. But there is also group karma, the collective debts of his group, and there are many groups: religions, races, nationalities, and so on. At a larger level, there is planetary karma, which will in time affect the planet's destiny and outcome. In group karma not only are individual debts accumulated and worked through, but the outcome is eventually applied to the group, country, or planet. The application of such group karma determines the future of the group or country. But it also applies to the reincarnating individual, both within the group or country, or simultaneously and intersecting but not within, or at a later point in time.

"Action becomes right action when it becomes action along the Way, along the Path toward God. All other paths are eventually blind alleys or illusions, and action along those paths is not right action. Thus right action promotes the individual's spirituality and his return. Action that fosters justice and mercy and love and wisdom and the attributes we call godly or spiritual is inevitably right action. The fruit of right action is the desired goal. The fruits of actions along the other paths are transient, illusory, and false. These fruits entrap and deceive, but they are not what we really desire. The fruits of right action encompass all our goals and wishes and all that we need or desire.

"Fame is an example. He that seeks fame as an end in itself may achieve fame for a while. But that fame will be temporary and will not gratify. If, however, fame comes to one unbidden, as a result of right action, action along the Path, that fame will endure and will be proper. But to the person on the Path, it will not matter. This is the difference between fame sought selfishly, for the individual, and fame unsought and not desired, a by-product of right action. The first is illusion and is impermanent. The second is real and permanent, adhering to the soul. The first accrues karma and must be balanced; the second does not."

Sometimes the messages flash by very quickly and succinctly.

"The goal is not to win but to open up."

Then, as if his/her turn came again, more from the psychological source and the rapid-fire impressions.

"God forgives, but you also have to be forgiven by people . . . and you have to forgive them. Forgiveness is also your responsibility. You must forgive and be forgiven. Psychoanalysis does not repair the damage. You still have to go beyond understanding and make *changes*, improve the world, repair relationships, forgive others and accept their forgiveness. Being active in seeking virtue is of the utmost importance. Lip service is not enough. Intellectual understanding without applying the remedy is not enough. Expressing your love is."

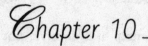

Chapter 10

I have been here before,
But when or how I cannot tell;
I know the grass beyond the door,
The sweet keen smell,
The sighing sound, the lights around the shore.
You have been mine before—
How long ago I may not know:
But just when at that swallow's soar
Your neck turned so,
Some veil did fall,—I knew it all of yore.

DANTE GABRIEL ROSSETTI

*P*edro entered the middle of a difficult lifetime. Sometimes the difficult ones offer the most opportunities to learn, opportunities to progress more quickly along our paths. Sometimes the relatively easy lifetimes offer fewer chances for advancement. They are times to rest. This was definitely not one of the easy ones. Immediately Pedro was angry, and he clenched his jaw tightly. "They're making me go, and I do not want to. . . . I do not wish that kind of life!"

"Where are they making you go?" I asked, looking for clarification.

"Into the priesthood, to be a monk. . . . I do not want this!" he said, insistently. He was silent for a moment, still angry. Then he began to explain.

"I am the youngest son. It is expected that I do this.

70

But I do not want to leave her. . . . We are in love; but if I go, someone else will have her, not me. . . . I cannot bear that. I would die first!"

But he did not die. Instead, he became gradually resigned to the inevitable. He had to separate from his love. His heart was ripped out, but he continued to live anyway.

Years passed.

"It is not so bad now. The life is peaceful. I am very attached to the abbot and I have chosen to stay with him. . . ." After more silence, a recognition.

"He is my brother . . . my brother. I know it is him. We are very close. I can see his eyes!"

Pedro had finally found his deceased brother. I knew that now his grief would begin to heal. The brothers had indeed been together before. And if before, they could be together again.

More years passed. The abbot grew old.

"He will leave me soon," Pedro predicted. "But we will be together again, in heaven. . . . We have prayed for that." The abbot soon died, and Pedro grieved.

He prayed and he meditated, and the time of his death approached. He had contracted tuberculosis and he was coughing. Breathing was difficult. His spiritual brothers stood around his bedside.

I let him pass quickly to the other side. There was no need to suffer again.

"I learned about anger and forgiveness," he began, not even waiting for me to ask about the lessons of that lifetime.

"I learned that anger is foolish. It eats at the soul. My parents did what they thought best, for me and for them. They did not understand the intensity of my passions or that I had the right to determine the direction of my life, not they. They meant well, but they did not understand. They were ignorant . . . but I have been ignorant also. I have commandeered the lives of others. So how can I judge them or be angry with them when I have done the same?"

He was silent again, then resumed. "This is why forgiveness is so important. We have all done those things for which we condemn others. If we want to be forgiven, we must forgive them. God forgives us. We should forgive, too." He was still reviewing the lessons.

"I would not have met the abbot if I had my way," he concluded. "There is always compensation, always grace, always goodness, if we just look for it. If I had remained angry and bitter, if I had resented my life, I would have missed the love and the goodness that I found in the monastery."

There were other, smaller lessons.

"I learned about the power of prayer and meditation," he added. He was silent again as he pondered the lessons and implications of that saintly life.

"Perhaps it was better to sacrifice romantic love," he conjectured, "for the greater love of God and my brothers."

I was not sure, and neither was he. Several hundred years later in Germany, Pedro's soul, in Magda, chose a very different path.

The next step in Pedro's journey to find the meeting point between spiritual love and romantic love occurred immediately after his memory of the monk.

"I'm being pulled back to another life," he announced abruptly. "I must go!"

"Go ahead," I urged. "What is happening?"

He was silent for a few moments.

"I'm lying on the ground, gravely wounded. . . . There are soldiers nearby. They have pulled me over the ground and the rocks. . . . I'm dying!" He gasped.

"My head and my side hurt badly," he muttered in a thin voice. "They are no longer interested in me."

The rest of this poor man's story slowly emerged. When he stopped responding, the soldiers left. He could see them above him in their short leather uniforms and boots. They were not happy. They were having their fun, but they had not really meant to kill him. They were not sad. These people were not worth very much. All in all, an unsatisfying escapade.

His daughter came to him, wailing and sobbing, and she softly cradled his head in her lap. She rocked rhythmically, and he could feel the life ebbing from his shattered body. His ribs must have been broken because there was a sharp pain with every breath. He tasted blood in his mouth.

His strength was diminishing rapidly now. He tried to speak to his daughter but could not utter a word. A distant gurgling came from somewhere in the depths of his body.

"I love you, father," he heard her say softly. He was too weak to answer. He loved her very much, this daughter. He would miss her beyond human endurance.

His eyes closed for the last time, and the incredible pain disappeared. Somehow he could still see. He felt extremely light and free. He found himself looking down at his crumpled body, his head and shoulders resting limply in his daughter's lap. She was sobbing, completely unaware that he was now at peace, that the pain was gone. She was focusing only on his body, a body that no longer held him, rocking slowly back and forth.

He could leave his family now, if he wanted. They would be all right. They only needed to remember that they would also leave their bodies when their time arrived.

He became aware of a marvelous light, brighter and more beautiful than a thousand suns. Yet he could look directly at it. Someone in or near the light was beckoning to him. His grandmother! She looked so young, so radiant, so healthy. He desired to go to her, and instantly he was with her near the light.

"It is good to see you again, my child," she thought, the words appearing in his consciousness. "It has been a long time."

She hugged him in arms of spirit, and they walked together into the light.

Pedro's haunting story completely engrossed me. Moved by his grief at leaving his daughter, I could feel the profound sadness of his parting words. However, I rejoiced at the uplifting encounter with his grandmother.

If I were not so overwhelmed by the emotions of the moment, which also evoked the tragic memory of my own son's death, perhaps my mind would have made the connection between Pedro and Elizabeth.

I had heard the daughter's words before. As Miriam, Elizabeth had rocked back and forth on the bloody ground, cradling her dying father, and she had whispered the same lament. The stories were eerily similar.

At that moment not only was my view obscured by emotion, but several weeks and dozens of other patients had intervened since Elizabeth's recounting, thus dimming my awareness even more.

The discovery of their entwined destinies would be delayed to a different day.

* * *

My mind flashed back to the short life of my firstborn son, Adam. I think it was my mental picture of the grief of Pedro's daughter in that ancient life that precipitated this memory.

Carole and I had rocked in each other's arms after the early-morning phone call from the doctor at the hospital. Adam's life had ended at twenty-three days. Heroic open-heart surgery could not save him. We cried, and we rocked. There was nothing else we could do at that moment.

Our grief seemed overwhelming, beyond physical and mental endurance. Even breathing became difficult. It hurt to take a deep breath, and air was hard to come by, as if there were a constricting corset around our chests, a corset of grief, but with no ties to undo.

With time the intensity and sharpness of our sadness slowly abated, but the hole in our hearts remained. We had Jordan, and we had Amy, and they are unique and special children, but they did not replace Adam.

The passage of time did help. Like ripples in a pond after a heavy stone disturbs its peaceful surface, waves of grief spread slowly outward. Like the first waves which tightly encircle the stone, everything in our lives was connected to Adam.

With time, new people and new experiences came into our lives. They were not as directly connected to Adam and to our pain. Ripples spreading ever outward. More new events, more new things, more new people. Breathing room. We could take deep breaths again. You never forget the hurt, but, as time passes, you can live around it.

We met Adam again ten years later in Miami. He talked

to us through Catherine, the patient described in *Many Lives, Many Masters*, and our lives were never the same. After a decade of pain, we began to understand about the immortality of souls.

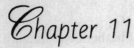

Chapter 11

> Many times man lives and dies
> Between his two eternities,
> That of race and that of soul,
> And ancient Ireland knew it all.
> Whether man die in his bed
> Or the rifle knocks him dead,
> A brief parting from those dear
> Is the worst man has to fear.
> Though grave-diggers' toil is long,
> Sharp their spades their muscles strong.
> They but thrust their buried men
> Back in the human mind again.
>
> W.B. YEATS

Elizabeth sobbed softly as she sat in the familiar recliner. Her mascara was running in jagged lines away from her eyes. I gave her a tissue, and she dabbed absentmindedly at her eyes as the black mascara lines gained speed in their descent toward her chin.

She had just finished recounting a life as an Irish woman, a life that had ended peacefully and with much happiness. Yet the stark contrast to her current life, with its losses and despair, was causing her pain. And so she cried, despite the happy ending. These were tears of sadness, not of joy.

The day's session had begun much less dramatically. Elizabeth had only recently regained the energy and self-confidence to enter into a relationship, this time a short-term encounter with an older man. Elizabeth was initially attracted to him because he had money and position. But there was no chemistry, at least not on her part. Her head urged her to settle, to accept that he was secure, he seemed to care for her quite a bit, and who else was there for her anyway?

Elizabeth's heart said no. Do not settle. You do not love him, and without love, what is there?

Her heart's argument finally won. He was pressing her to deepen the relationship, to have sex, to make commitments. Elizabeth decided to end it. She was relieved, sad to be lonely again, but not depressed. Overall, she was handling the end of this relationship very appropriately. And yet here she was, eyes red, nose stuffy, mascara running wildly.

When we started the regression process, Elizabeth lapsed into a deep trance, and I took her back in time once again. This time she emerged in Ireland, several centuries ago.

"I'm very pretty," she commented immediately upon finding herself. "I have dark hair and light blue eyes. . . . I dress very plainly and wear no makeup or jewelry . . . as if I'm hiding. My skin is so white, like cream."

"Hiding from what?" I inquired, following her lead.

She was silent for a few moments, looking for the answer. "From my husband . . . yes, from him. Oh, he's a lout! He drinks too much, and he becomes violent. . . . He's so selfish. . . . I curse this marriage!"

"Why did you choose him?" I innocently asked.

"I did *not* choose him. . . . I would *never* choose him. My parents chose him, and now they are dead. . . . They are dead, but I still have to live with him. He is all I have now," she said, a fragile sadness joining the anger in her voice.

"Do you have any children? Does anyone else live with you?" I asked.

"No." Her anger was subsiding, but the sadness was more evident now. "I cannot. I had a . . . miscarriage. There was a great deal of bleeding . . . and infection. They say I can't bear children. . . . He is angry at me for that, too. . . . He blames me . . . for not bearing him sons. As if I *wanted* this!" She was upset again.

"He hits me," she added, in a suddenly soft voice. "He hits me as if I were a dog. I hate him for that." She stopped talking and tears formed in the corners of her eyes.

"He hits you?" I echoed.

"Yes," she answered simply.

I waited for more, but she was reluctant to elaborate. "Where does he hit you?" I pressed.

"On my back, my arms, my face. Everywhere."

"Can you stop him?"

"At times. I used to hit back, but then he hurts me more. He drinks too much. The best thing I can do is accept the beating. Eventually he tires and stops . . . until the next time."

"Look at him closely," I urged her. "Look into his eyes. See if you recognize him as anyone in your current life."

Elizabeth's eyes narrowed, and her brow furrowed, as if she were looking, even though her eyelids remained closed.

"I *do* know him! It's George. . . . It's George!"

"Good. You are back in that lifetime. The beatings have stopped."

She had recognized the banker, George, with whom she had had a relationship a year and a half earlier. That relationship had ended when George became physically abusive.

Patterns such as abusiveness can persist over many lifetimes if they are not recognized and broken. At some subconscious level Elizabeth and George had remembered each other. They had come together once again, and he tried to resume the abuse. However, Elizabeth had learned an important lesson over the centuries. This time Elizabeth had the strength and self-respect to end their relationship soon after the abuse began. When past-life origins are discovered, it is even easier to break destructive patterns.

I looked over at Elizabeth. She was quiet. She seemed so sad and hopeless. I had enough information about her abusive husband, and I decided to move her ahead in time.

"I will count backward from three to one and tap you lightly on the forehead," I told her. "As I do this, move ahead to the next significant event in this life. Let it come into complete focus in your mind as I count. See what happens to you."

On the count of one, she began to smile blissfully. I was glad there was a little light in this bleak life.

"He has died, thank God, and I am so happy," she gushed. "I am with a man I love. He is so kind and gentle. He never hits me. We love each other. He's a very good man. We are happy together." Her blissful smile never faded.

"How did your husband die?" I inquired.

"In a tavern," she answered, as her smile faded. "He was killed in a fight. They tell me that he was stabbed in the chest with a long knife. It must have pierced his heart. They tell me blood was everywhere.

"I am not sad that he died," she continued. "I would not have met John otherwise. John is a wonderful man." Her radiant smile had returned.

Once again I pressed forward. "Go ahead in time," I instructed, "and see what happens to you and John. Go to the next significant event in your lives."

She was silent, scanning the years.

"I am very weak. My heart is fluttering so," she gasped. "I cannot catch my breath!" She had progressed to the day of her death.

"Is John around?" I asked.

"Oh, yes. He's sitting on the bed and holding my hand. He's very concerned, very attentive. He knows he's going to lose me. We are sad about this but happy that we lived so many good years together." She paused, remembering the scene with John at her bedside. Only Elizabeth's relationship with her beloved mother had approached this incredible level of love, joy, and intimacy she had shared with John.

"Look closely at John. Look at his face and in his eyes. See if you recognize him as someone in your present life." Recognition often immediately occurs with an unmistakable certainty when a patient looks into the other person's eyes. The eyes may truly be the window to the soul.

"No," she said simply. "I do not know him."

She paused again, then spoke with alarm in her voice.

"My heart is giving out," she declared. "It's very erratic now. I feel like I want to leave this body now."

"It's okay. Leave that body. Tell me what happens to you."

After a few moments, she began to describe the events following her death. Her face looked peaceful, her breathing relaxed.

"I am hovering above and to the side of my body, near the corner of the ceiling. I can see John sitting with my body. He's just sitting there. He doesn't want to move. He will be all alone now. We only had each other."

"Then you never had children?" I asked, for clarification.

"No, I could not. But that was not important. We had each other, and that was enough for us." She lapsed back into silence, her face still very peaceful, a small smile forming.

"It is so beautiful here. I am aware of a beautiful light all around me. It pulls at me, and I want to follow it. It is a beautiful light. It restores you with energy!"

"Go ahead," I agreed.

"We travel through a beautiful valley, with trees and flowers all around. . . . I am becoming aware of many things, much information, much knowledge. But I don't want to forget about John. I *must* remember John, and if I learn all these other things, I might forget John, and I can't!"

"You will remember John, too," I advised, but I was not really sure. What was this other knowledge she was being given? I asked her.

"It is all about lifetimes and energies, about how we use our lifetimes to perfect our energies so that we can move on to higher worlds. They are telling me about energy and about love and how these are the same . . . when we understand what love *really* is. But I do not want to forget about John!"

"I will remind you all about John."

"Good."

"Is there more?"

"No, that is all for now. . . ." Then she added, "We can learn more about love by listening to our intuitions."

Perhaps this last comment had more levels of meaning, especially for me. Years earlier the Masters, speaking through Catherine, had told me at the very end of her sessions and their amazing revelations, "What we tell you is for now. You must now learn through your own intuition." There would be no more revelations through Catherine's hypnosis.

Elizabeth rested. There would be no further revelations today either. I awakened her, and after her mind reoriented to the present time, she began to cry softly.

"Why are you crying?" I gently asked her.

"Because I loved him so much, and I don't think I will ever love someone that much again. I've never met any man that I could love like that, and who loved me back the same way. And without that love, how can my life ever be complete? How can I ever be completely happy?"

"You never know," I objected, but without much conviction. "You *could* meet someone and fall madly in love again. You could even meet John again, in another body."

"Sure," she said with some sarcasm. Her tears kept falling. "You're just trying to make me feel better. I've got a better chance of winning the lottery than of finding him again."

The odds of winning the lottery, I remembered, were fourteen million to one.

★ ★ ★

In *Through Time into Healing*, I describe the reunion of Ariel and Anthony.

A reunion with a soulmate after a long and involuntary separation can be an experience worth waiting for—even if the wait is one of centuries.

On a vacation in the Southwest, my former patient, Ariel, a biologist, met an Australian named Anthony. Both were emotionally mature individuals who had been married before, and they quickly fell in love and became engaged. Back in Miami, Ariel suggested that Anthony have a regression session with me just to see if he could have the experience and to "see what came up." They were both curious to find out whether Ariel would appear in any way in Anthony's regression.

Anthony turned out to be a superb regression subject. Almost instantly, he returned to a very vivid North African lifetime around the time of Hannibal, more than two thousand years ago. In that lifetime, Anthony had been a member of a very advanced civilization. His particular tribe was fair skinned, and they were gold smelters who had the ability to use liquid fire as a weapon by spreading it on the surface of rivers. Anthony was a young man in his mid-twenties in the midst of fighting a forty-day war with a neighboring, darker-skinned tribe that vastly outnumbered the defenders.

Anthony's tribe had actually trained some of the members of the enemy tribe in the art of warfare, and one of the former trainees was leading the assault. One hundred thousand of the enemy tribe carrying swords and hatchets were crossing a large river on ropes as Anthony and his people spread liquid fire on their own river, hoping it would reach the attackers before the attackers reached the shore.

To protect their women and children, the defending tribe put most of them on large boats with violet sails in the middle of a huge lake. Among this group was Anthony's young and beloved fiancée, who was perhaps seventeen or eighteen years old. However, the liquid fire suddenly burned out of control, and the boats caught fire. Most of the tribe's women and children perished in this tragic accident, including Anthony's fiancée, who was his great passion.

This tragedy broke the morale of the warriors, and they were soon defeated. Anthony was one of the few who escaped the slaughter through brutal hand-to-hand fighting. Eventually, he escaped to a secret passageway that led to a warren of rooms underneath the large temple where the tribe's treasures were stored.

There Anthony had found one other living person, his king. The king commanded Anthony to kill him, and Anthony, a loyal soldier, complied against his will. After the king's death, Anthony was all alone in the dark temple, where he used his time to write the history of his people on gold leaf and to seal the writing in large urns or jars. It was here that he eventually died of starvation and grief over the loss of his fiancée and his people.

There was one more detail. His fiancée in that lifetime reincarnated as Ariel in this lifetime. The two of them reunited as lovers after two thousand years. Finally, the long-postponed wedding would take place.

Anthony and Ariel had only been separated for one hour when he stepped out of my office. But the power of their reunion was such that it was as though they had not seen each other for two thousand years.

Recently Ariel and Anthony were married. Their sudden and intense and seemingly coincidental meeting now has a new layer of meaning to them, and their already passionate relationship is now infused with a sense of continuous adventure.

Anthony and Ariel plan to take a trip to North Africa to try and find the location of their past life together and to see what other details they can uncover. They know that whatever they find can only increase the adventure they find in each other.

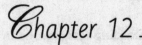

Chapter 12

> *Though I may not be a king in my future life, so much the better: I shall nevertheless live an active life and, on top of it, earn less ingratitude.*
>
> FREDERICK THE GREAT

He was perspiring profusely now, for the second time, despite the heavy air-conditioning in my office. Sweat poured down his face, drenched his shirt, rolled down his neck. A moment ago he had shaking chills and his body shivered. But malaria could do that, alternating bone-chilling cold and inflaming heat. Francisco was dying from this dreaded disease, alone and thousands of miles from his loved ones. It was a terrible, painful way to die.

Pedro had begun this office visit by drifting into a deeply relaxed, hypnotic state. He quickly went back through time and space, into a past lifetime, and immediately he began to sweat. I tried to dry his face with tissues, but it was like trying to stop a flood with one's hands. The sweat kept pouring down. I hoped that any physical discomfort cased by the drenching sweat would not affect the depth and intensity of his trance state.

"I'm a man . . . with black hair and tanned skin," he

gasped through the sweat. "I am unloading a large wooden ship . . . *heavy* cargo. . . . It's boiling hot here. . . . I see palm trees and flimsy wooden structures nearby. . . . I'm a sailor. . . . We are in the New World."

"Do you know the name?" I inquired.

"Francisco . . . my name is Francisco. I am a sailor."

I had meant the name of the place, but he had become aware of his name in that lifetime.

"Do you know the name of this place?" I asked again.

He paused for a moment, still sweating profusely. "I don't see that," he answered. "One of these accursed ports. . . . There is gold here. In the jungle . . . somewhere in the distant mountains. We will find it. . . . I can keep some of what I find. . . . This accursed place!"

"Where are you from?" I asked, looking for more details. "Do you know where your home is?"

"On the other side of the sea," he answered patiently. "In Spain . . . where we are from." He was including his fellow sailors, unloading a ship's cargo in the broiling sun.

"Do you have family in Spain?" I inquired.

"My wife and my son are there. . . . I miss them, but they are all right . . . especially with the gold I send back. My mother and my sisters are there, too. It's not an easy life. . . . I miss them greatly."

I wanted to learn more about his family.

"I am going to take you back in time," I told him, "back to your family in Spain, to the last time you were together, before this current journey to the New World. I will tap you on your forehead and count backward from three to one. When I reach one, you will be back in Spain with your family. You can remember everything.

"Three . . . two . . . one. Be there!"

Pedro's eyes were moving under closed lids as he scanned a scene.

"I can see my wife and my small son. We are sitting to eat. . . . I see the wooden table and chairs. . . . My mother is there also," he observed.

"Look into their faces, into their eyes," I instructed. "See if you recognize them as anyone in your current life." I was concerned that shifting between lifetimes could be disorienting and might pop Pedro entirely out of Francisco's time. But he handled it smoothly.

"I recognize my son. He is my brother. . . . Oh yes, he is Juan . . . how beautiful!" He had found his brother before, as the abbot, when Pedro was a monk. Although we had never found them as lovers, Juan was an enduring soulmate for Pedro. Their soul connection was wonderfully close.

He ignored his mother, focusing completely on his young wife.

"We love each other deeply," he commented. "But I don't recognize her from this life. Our love is very strong."

He was silent for a while, enjoying the memory of his young wife and the deep love that they had shared four or five hundred years ago in a Spain so much different from today's.

Would Pedro ever taste this kind of love? Did the soul of Francisco's wife also cross the centuries to be here again, and, if so, would they ever meet?

I took Francisco back to the New World and the search for gold.

"Go back to the port," I instructed, "where you have been unloading the ship. Now move ahead in time to the next significant event in that sailor's life. As I count backward from three to one and tap your forehead, let it all come into focus—the next significant event."

"Three . . . two . . . one. You are there."

Francisco started to shiver.

"I'm so cold," he complained. "But I *know* that infernal fever will return!" As predicted, a few moments later the heavy sweating began anew.

"Damn!" he cursed. "This will kill me, this sickness . . . and the others have left me behind. . . . They know I cannot keep up. . . . They know there is no hope for me. . . . I am doomed in this God-forsaken place. We didn't even find the treasures of gold they swear is here."

"Do you survive this illness?" I gently asked.

He was quiet, and we waited. "I died from this. I never leave the jungle. . . . The fever kills me, and I never see my family again. They will be very grieved. . . . My son is so young." The sweat on Pedro's face was now mixed with his tears. He was grieving his early death, alone in an alien land, from a strange disease that no sailor's skill could defeat.

I had him detach from Francisco's body, and he floated in a state of calm and tranquillity, freed from the fever and pain, beyond grief and suffering. His face was much more peaceful and relaxed, and I let him rest.

I pondered this pattern of losses in Pedro's lifetimes. So many separations from his loved ones. So much grief. As he made his way through the uncertain and nebulous mists of time, would he be able to find them again? Would he find all of them?

Pedro's lifetimes contained many patterns, not just losses. In this regression, he remembered being a Spaniard, but he had also been an English soldier, killed by the Spanish enemy when his forces invaded their fortress.

He remembered being male, and he remembered being female. He had experienced lifetimes as a warrior and lifetimes as a priest. He had lost people, and he had found them.

After he had died as a monk, surrounded by his spiritual family, Pedro had reviewed the lessons of that lifetime.

"Forgiveness is so important," he had told me. "We have all done those things for which we condemn others. . . . We must forgive them."

His lives illustrated his message. He had to learn from all sides in order to truly understand. We all do. We change religions, races, and nationalities. We experience lifetimes of extreme wealth and of abject poverty, of sickness and of health.

We must learn to reject all prejudice and hatred. Those who do not will simply switch sides, returning in the bodies of their enemies.

In his song "Tears in Heaven," Eric Clapton wonders whether his young son, who had tragically died in an accident, would know his name if they met in heaven.

His is a universal and ageless question. How will we recognize our loved ones? Will we know them, and will they know us, if and when we meet again, whether in heaven or on earth, once more in physical bodies?

Many of my patients just seem to know. When experiencing their past lives, they look into a soul companion's eyes, and they know. Whether in heaven or on earth, they sense a vibration or energy, and it is the same as their loved one's. They glimpse the deeper personality, and there is an inner knowing—a knowing from the heart. A connection is made.

Because it is the heart's eyes that often see first, words

alone cannot convey the confidence of soul recognition. There is no wavering or confusion. Even though the body may be very different from the current one, the soul is the same. The soul is recognized, and the recognition is complete and beyond any doubt.

Sometimes soul recognition may originate in the mind and may occur even before the heart sees. This type of recognition happens most often with babies or young children. They exhibit some physical mannerism or unique behavior, they utter a word or phrase, and a beloved parent or grandparent is instantly recognized. They may have an identical scar or birthmark as your loved one or perhaps just hold your hand or look at you in that same special way. You know.

In heaven, there are no birthmarks. Would Eric Clapton's son help him there, the song asks. Would he hold Eric's hand? Would he help him stand?

In heaven, where physical bodies are not needed, soul recognition may occur through an inner knowing, a sense of a loved one's special energy, light, or vibration. You *feel* them, in you heart. There is a deep and intuitive wisdom there, and you recognize them completely and immediately. They may even help you by assuming the body they had during their last incarnation with you. You see them as they appeared to you on earth, often younger and healthier.

Clapton concludes that he will find peace beyond heaven's door.

Whether beyond the door to heaven, the door to remembering past lifetimes together, or the door leading to future lifetimes with your loved ones, you will never be alone. They will know your name. They will hold your hand. They will bring peace and healing to your heart.

Over and over, my patients, while deeply hypnotized, tell me that death is not an accident. When babies and young children die, we are given the opportunity to learn important lessons. They are teachers to us, teaching us about values, priorities, and, most of all, about love.

Often the most important lessons arise from the most difficult times.

Chapter 13 _____

Our birth is but a sleep and a forgetting;
The Soul that rises with us, our life's star,
Hath had elsewhere its setting,
And cometh from afar,
Not in entire forgetfulness
And not in utter nakedness,
But trailing clouds of glory do we come
From God who is our home.
Heaven lies about us in our infancy!

WILLIAM WORDSWORTH

Despite her success in recalling several past lives, Elizabeth still ached with grief. Intellectually, she had begun to accept the concept of the continuity of the soul and the recurrence of consciousness in subsequent physical bodies. She had experienced the reunion of soul companions along this journey. But memories did not bring her mother back, not *physically*. She could not hug her and talk to her. She missed her mother dearly.

As Elizabeth came into the office for today's session, I decided to try something different, something I had done with varying degrees of success with other patients. As usual, I would help her achieve a state of deep relaxation. I would then guide her in visualizing a beautiful garden, have her walk into the garden, and rest. As she was resting, I would suggest that a visitor was joining her in the garden and that Elizabeth could communicate with this visitor in thoughts, voice, vision, feelings, or in any other way.

Everything that Elizabeth experienced after this point would come from her own mind, not from my suggestions.

She sank deeply into the familiar leather recliner and quickly entered the tranquil hypnotic state. I counted backward from ten to one, deepening her level even more. She imagined herself walking down a spiral staircase. As she reached the bottom of the steps, she visualized the garden in front of her. She walked into the garden and found a place to rest. I told her about the visitor, and we waited.

After a short while, she became aware that a beautiful light was approaching her. In the quiet office, Elizabeth began to cry softly.

"Why are you crying?" I questioned.

"It's my mother. . . . I can see her in the light. She looks so beautiful, so young."

Now speaking directly to her mother, she added, "It's so good to see you." Elizabeth was smiling and crying at the same time.

"You can talk to her; you can communicate with her," I reminded Elizabeth. I did not say anything more at this point as I didn't want to interfere with the reunion. Elizabeth was not recalling a memory, nor was she re-experiencing some event that had already occurred. This experience was happening now.

The meeting with her mother was taking place vividly and emotionally in Elizabeth's mind. That their reunion existed so powerfully in her mind conferred a considerable degree of reality to her experience. The potential to help her heal her grief was now present.

We sat quietly for several minutes, the silence sometimes punctuated by small sighs. At times I could see a
tear roll down Elizabeth's cheek. She smiled frequently.
Finally, she began to speak.

"She is gone now," Elizabeth said very calmly. "She had
to go, but she will be back." Elizabeth remained deeply
relaxed with her eyes still closed as we continued to talk.

"Did she communicate with you?" I asked.

"Yes, she told me many things. She told me to trust
in myself. She said, 'Trust in yourself. I have taught you
everything you need to know!' "

"What does this mean to you?"

"That I must believe in my own feelings and not let
others influence me all the time . . . especially *men*," she
replied emphatically.

"She said that men have taken advantage of me because
I didn't believe in myself enough, and I let them. I gave
them too much power, robbing myself at the same time.
I must stop doing this.

" 'We are all the same,' she told me. 'Souls are not
male or female. You are as beautiful and as powerful as
any other soul in the universe. Do not forget this; do not
become distracted by their physical forms.' This is what
she said."

"Did she tell you anything else?"

"Yes, there is more," she answered, but did not elaborate.

"What?" I prodded.

"That she loves me dearly," Elizabeth added in a delicate way. "That she is fine. She is helping many souls on
the other side. . . . She will still always be there for me. . . .
There was one more thing."

"What is that?"

"To be patient. Something will happen very soon, something important. And I must trust in myself."

"What will happen?"

"I don't know," she answered softly. "But when it does, I will trust myself," she added with a resolve I had never noticed in her before.

Sitting in the green room of the "Donahue" show, I witnessed a stunningly surrealistic scene. There was Jenny Cockell, a forty-one-year-old woman from England, sitting with her son, Sonny, age seventy-five, and her daughter, Phyllis, who was sixty-nine years old at the time. Their story is far better and more convincing than Bridey Murphy's, a famous landmark reincarnation case.

Ever since her early childhood, Jenny knew that in a recent past life she had died suddenly, leaving her eight children virtual orphans. She knew detailed facts about their early-twentieth-century lives in rural Ireland. Her name in that life was Mary.

Jenny's family humored her, but there were not enough funds or interest to investigate the child's fantastic stories of a life of crushing poverty and tragedy in Ireland decades ago. Jenny grew up not knowing if her vivid recollections were real or not.

Finally, Jenny had the resources to begin her research. She found five of the eight children of Mary Sutton, an Irish woman who died in 1932 from complications after the birth of her eighth child. Mary Sutton's children confirmed many of Jenny's incredibly detailed memories. They seemed convinced that Jenny was indeed Mary, their "dead" mother.

And I was watching their ongoing reunion, there in the green room of the "Donahue" show.

My mind shifted gears and I saw the beginning sequence of the old "Ben Casey" television show. This was a medical show in the late fifties or early sixties. My mother, in her subtle way, encouraged me to watch this program, relentlessly influencing me to choose medicine as my career.

The "Ben Casey" show always began with universal symbols, and the aged neurosurgeon mentor of the young Dr. Ben Casey intoned, "Man . . . Woman . . . Birth . . . Death . . . Infinity." Or something very much like this. Universal mysteries, unanswerable riddles. Sitting in the green room just prior to going on "Donahue" as an expert on past-life memories, I was *getting the answers* that had eluded young Ben Casey and all the others.

Man? Woman? In the course of our lifetimes, we change sexes, religions, and races in order to learn from all sides. We are all in school here. Birth? If we never really die, then we are never really born. We are all immortal, divine, and indestructible. Death is nothing more than walking through a door into another room. We keep returning in order to learn certain lessons, or traits, such as love . . . forgiveness . . . understanding . . . patience . . . awareness . . . nonviolence. . . . We have to unlearn other traits, such as fear . . . anger . . . greed . . . hatred . . . pride . . . ego . . . which result from old conditioning. Then we can graduate and leave this school. We have all the time in the world to learn and unlearn. We are immortal; we are infinite; we have the nature of God.

As I watched Jenny and her aged children, even more came to me.

"Whatsoever a man soweth, that shall he also reap." The concept of karma is stated virtually word for word in all the great religions. This wisdom is ancient. We are responsible to ourselves, to others, to the community, and to the planet.

Propelled by her need to care for and to protect her children, Jenny was pulled back to them once again. We never lose our loved ones. We keep coming back, together and together again. What a powerful reuniting energy love is.

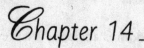

Chapter 14 _____

My doctrine is: Live so that thou mayest desire to live again—that is thy duty—for in any case thou wilt again!

NIETZSCHE

$\mathscr{T}$here are many bridges, or techniques, for helping a patient remember past lives through hypnosis. One of these bridges is a door. Often I will put patients into a deep hypnotic trance and have them walk through a door they choose, a door into a past lifetime. "Imagine yourself standing in a beautiful corridor or hallway, with large and magnificent doors on either side and at the ends. These are doorways into your past, even into your past lives. They may lead you to spiritual experiences. As I count backward from five to one, one of these doors will open, a door to your past. This door will pull you. It will attract you. Go to it.

"Five. The door is opening. This door will help you to understand any blocks or obstacles to joy and happiness in your current life. Go to the door.

"Four. You are at the door. You see a beautiful light on the other side of the door. Step through the door and into the light.

"Three. Go through the light. You are in another time and another place.

"Do not worry about what is imagination, fantasy, actual memory, symbol, metaphor, or some combination of all of these. It is the experience that matters. Just let yourself experience whatever pops into your mind. Try not to think, judge, or critique. Just let yourself experience. Whatever comes into your awareness is fine. You can analyze it later.

"Two. Nearly there, nearly through the light. When I say 'One,' be there and join the person or scene on the other side of the light. Let it all come into focus on the count of one.

"One! Be there. Look at your feet and see what kind of footwear you are wearing. Look at your clothes, your skin, your hands. Are they the same or different? Pay attention to details."

The door is just one of many bridges to the past. All lead to the same place, to a past life or a spiritual experience that is important to the person's current life situation. Elevators traveling back through time; a road or pathway or even an actual bridge through the mists of time; stepping across a creek, brook, stream, or small river to the other side, to another lifetime; a time machine, with the patient operating the control panel—these are just a few examples of the myriad pathways or bridges to the past. For Pedro, I used the doorways.

When he tried to look at his feet after emerging from the light, he found himself staring instead at the large stone mask of a god.

"He has a long nose and large angled teeth. The mouth . . . lips . . . are strange, very large and wide. His eyes are round and set deeply and far apart. He has a very mean look. . . . The gods can be cruel."

"How do you know this is a god?"

"He is very powerful."

"Are there many gods, or is he the only one?"

"There are many, but he is a powerful one. . . . He controls the rain. Without rain we could not grow food," Pedro explained simply.

"Are you there? Can you find yourself?" I urged.

"I'm there. I'm a priest of some sort. I know about the heavens and the sun, moon, and stars. I help to make the calendars."

"Where do you do this work?"

"In a building made of stone. It has stairs that circle around and small windows through which we see and measure. It's very complicated, but I'm good at this. They rely on me for the measurements. . . . I know when the eclipses will occur."

"It sounds as if this is a very scientific civilization," I commented.

"Only parts of it, the astronomy and the architecture. The rest is superstitious and backward," he clarified. "There are other priests and their supporters who are only interested in power. They use superstitions and fear to delude the people and maintain their power. They are supported by nobles who help to control the warriors. It's an alliance to keep power in the hands of only a few."

The time and the culture Pedro remembered may have been ancient, but the techniques of control and the political alliances formed to gain and maintain power are timeless. The ambitions of men never seem to change.

"How do they use superstitions to delude the people?"

"They blame the gods for natural events. Then they blame the people for angering or displeasing the gods . . . so the people become responsible for natural events, like floods or droughts or earthquakes or volcanic eruptions. When the people are not to blame at all . . . and neither the gods. . . . These are events of nature and *not* the actions of angry gods . . . but the people do not realize this. They stay ignorant and fearful—fearful because they feel responsible for these calamities." Pedro paused for a few moments, then he continued.

"It's a mistake to externalize our problems, our calamities, to the gods. This gives the priests and nobles too much power. . . . We understand more about natural events than the people do. We usually know when they begin and when they end. We understand about the cycles. An eclipse is a natural event that can be calculated and predicted. It's not an act of anger or punishment by the gods . . . but that is what they tell the people." Pedro was speaking rapidly now; words and concepts poured from him without my prodding.

"The priests hold themselves out as the communicators to the gods. They tell the people they are the only intermediaries, that they know what the gods want. I know this is not true. . . . I am one of the priests." He thought silently for a moment.

"Go on," I suggested.

"The priests have developed a cruel and elaborate system of sacrifices to appease the gods." His voice dropped to a whisper. "Even sacrifices of people."

"Of people?" I echoed.

"Yes," he whispered. "They do not have to do this often, because it strikes such fear into the people. There are rituals for drowning and rituals for slaying. . . . As if gods need human blood!" Pedro's voice was rising as anger crept in. "They manipulate the people with rituals of fear. They even choose who is to be sacrificed. This gives them as much power as their gods. They choose who is to live and who must die."

"Do you have to take part in the ritual sacrifices?" I cautiously asked him.

"No," he answered. "I do not believe in them. They let me stay with my observations and calculations."

"I do not even believe that these gods exist," he whispered in a confidential way.

"You don't?"

"No. How can gods be as petty and foolish as people? When I observe the heaven and the beautiful harmony of the sun and moon, the planets and the stars . . . how can such an intelligence, such a wisdom, be petty and foolish at the same time? It makes no sense. We give these so-called gods our own qualities. Fear, anger, jealousy, hatred—these are ours and we project them onto these gods. I believe the real god is far beyond human emotions. The real god does not need our rituals and sacrifices."

This ancient incarnation of Pedro possessed great wisdom. He talked easily, even of taboo subjects, and he did not seem tired, so I decided to press ahead.

"Do you ever become more influential as a priest?" I asked. "Do you gain more power in that lifetime?"

"No, I don't," he responded. "I would not rule like that if I had power. I would educate the people. I would let them learn for themselves. I would stop the sacrifices."

"But the priests and nobles might lose their power," I objected. "What if the people stopped listening?"

"They would not," he said. "Real power comes from knowledge. Real wisdom is applying that knowledge in a caring and benevolent manner. The people are ignorant, but that can change. They are not stupid."

The priest was teaching me about spiritual politics, and I could feel the truth in his words.

"Go on," I requested, after another period of silence.

"There is no more," Pedro answered. "I have left that body, and I am resting."

This surprised me. I had not asked him to leave. We had not experienced a death scene, and there was no jarring or traumatic event that might have spontaneously dislodged him. I remembered that he had entered this lifetime in an unusual way, confronting the huge stone face of the god of rain.

Perhaps there was nothing more to be gained from examining that lifetime any further, and Pedro's higher mind knew this. And so he left.

He would have been a marvelous ruler.

In November of 1992, Galileo was exonerated by the Church for his "accursed heresy," which held that the earth was not the nucleus of the universe but that in fact the earth revolved around the sun. The investigation that cleared Galileo began in 1980 and lasted for twelve and one-half years. The work of the Inquisition in 1633 was finally undone three hundred and fifty-nine years later. Unfortunately, closed-mindedness is often undone even more slowly.

All institutions seem to be closed-minded. Individuals who never question their assumptions and belief systems are similarly closed-minded. How can they assimilate new observations and new knowledge when their minds are blinded by beliefs and by untested old ideas?

Years ago, while in a deep trance state, Catherine told me, "Our task is to learn, to become God-like through knowledge. We know so little. . . . By knowledge we approach God, and then we can rest. Then we come back to teach and help others."

Knowledge can only flow into minds that are open.

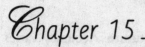

Chapter 15 _____

*I know I am deathless. No doubt I have died myself
ten thousand times before. I laugh at what you call
dissolution, and I know the amplitude of time.*

WALT WHITMAN

Dreams have many functions. They help to process and
integrate the day's events. They provide clues, often in
the form of symbols and metaphors, that help solve the
problems of everyday life—relationships, fears, work,
emotions, illnesses, and much more. They can assist us
in achieving our desires and goals if not physically then
at least in the form of wish fulfillment. They aid us in
reviewing past events, reminding us of parallels in the
present. They protect sleep by disguising stimuli such as
anxieties that would otherwise awaken us. Dreams have
deeper functions as well. They may provide pathways to
recovering repressed or forgotten memories, whether
from childhood, infancy, in-utero experiences, or even
from past lives. Past-life memory fragments often emerge
in the dream state, particularly in those dreams in which
the dreamer sees scenes from the years or centuries preced-
ing his or her birth.

Dreams can be psychic or precognitive. Often these

particular dreams can predict the future. Accuracy varies because the future appears to be a system of probabilities and inevitabilities, and because the ability of people to accurately interpret their dreams itself varies tremendously. These psychic or precognitive dreams are experienced by many people of all cultures and backgrounds. However, many people are shocked when their dreams literally come true.

Another type of psychic dream occurs when communication with a person at a distance is experienced. The person may be alive and geographically distant, or the communication may be with the soul or consciousness of someone who has died, such as a relative or dear friend. Similarly, there may be communication with an angelic spirit, a teacher, or a guide. The messages in these dreams are usually genuinely moving and very important.

"Traveling" dreams also occur. During these dreams people have the experience of visiting places to which they have never physically been. Details of what they see can later be confirmed. When the person actually visits the geographical place, even months or years after the dream, a feeling of déjà vu or familiarity may occur.

Sometimes the dream traveler visits places that do not seem to exist on this planet. These dreams may be far more than nocturnal imaginings. They may be mystical or spiritual experiences, accessed because the usual ego and cognitive barriers are relaxed during sleep and dreaming. Knowledge and wisdom acquired during this type of traveling dream can transform lives.

On this day, when night lightened into morning, Elizabeth had one of these dreams.

★　★　★

Elizabeth bounced in early for her appointment, eager to tell me about the dream she had during the previous night. She appeared less anxious and more relaxed than I had ever seen her. People at work, she told me, had begun to comment that she looked better, that she was being nicer and more patient, even more so than the "old" Elizabeth, before her mother's death.

"This was not one of my typical dreams," she stressed. "This dream was more alive and real. I still remember all the details, and I usually forget most of my dreams pretty quickly, as you know."

I had been encouraging Elizabeth to write down her dreams as soon as she awakened. Keeping a dream journal near your bed and jotting down what you remember of your dreams significantly enhances the memory. Otherwise the dream content fades rapidly away. Elizabeth had been somewhat lazy about chronicling her dreams, and by the time she came to the office for her appointment, she had usually forgotten most of the details, if not the entire dream.

This dream was different, so vivid that the details were etched in her mind.

"At first, I entered a large room. There were no windows or lamps or overhead lights. But the walls were somehow glowing. They emitted enough light to illuminate the entire room."

"Were the walls hot?" I asked.

"I don't think so. They gave off light but not heat. I didn't touch the walls though."

"What else did you notice in the room?"

"I knew it was a library of some sort, but I couldn't see any shelves or any books. In the corner of the room was a statue of the Sphinx. There were two old chairs on either side of this statue, old from an olden time. They were not from modern times. Almost like a throne made out of stone or marble." She was quiet for a moment, her gaze drifting upward and to the left as she remembered the ancient chairs.

"What do you think a statue of the Sphinx was doing there?" I inquired.

"I don't know. Maybe because the library helped you to understand secrets. I remembered the riddle of the Sphinx. What walks on four legs in the morning, two legs during the day, and three legs at night? Man does. A crawling baby becomes an adult who becomes elderly, needing a cane to walk. Maybe it has something to do with that riddle. Or with riddles in general."

"It could be," I conceded, my mind drifting back to *Oedipus* and the first time I had heard about the riddle.

"Yet there may be other meanings, too," I added. "For example, what if the Sphinx somehow provides a clue to the nature of the library, or even to its structure or its location?" The dreaming mind could be very complex.

"I wasn't there long enough to find out," she answered.

"Are you aware of anything else in the room?"

"Yes," she said immediately. "There was a man nearby, dressed in a long, white robe. I guess he was the librarian. He decided who could come into the room and who could not. For some reason, I was allowed in."

At this point my practical mind could not contain itself any longer.

"What kind of library doesn't have books?" I blurted out.

"That's the strange part," she began to explain. "All I had to do was to put my arms out with my palms up and whatever book I needed began to form right in my hands! In no time the book was complete. It seemed to come right out of the wall and solidify in my hands."

"What kind of book did you receive?"

"I don't remember exactly. A book about me, about my lifetimes. I was afraid to open it."

"Afraid of what?"

"I don't know. That there was something bad there, something I would be ashamed of."

"Did the librarian help you?"

"Not really. He just began to laugh. Then he said, 'Is a rose ashamed of its thorns?' And he laughed some more."

"Then what happened?"

"He led me out, but I felt that eventually I would understand what he meant and I would come back and not be afraid to read from my book." She grew silent, pensive.

"Was that the end of the dream?" I prodded.

"No. After leaving the library I went to a classroom where I was taking a course. There were fifteen or twenty other students there. One young man seemed very familiar, like he was my brother . . . but he wasn't my brother, Charles." She was referring to her present-life brother in California.

"What kind of a course were you taking?"

"I don't know."

"Was there more?" I asked.

She responded hesitantly. "Yes."

I wondered why she hesitated now, after already relating some very unusual dream scenes.

"A teacher appeared," she continued, in a voice slightly more than a whisper. "He had the most intense brown eyes. His eyes would change to a beautiful purple color, then back to brown again. He was very tall and wore only a white robe. His feet were bare. . . . He came to me and looked deeply into my eyes."

"Then what?"

"I felt the most incredible love. I knew that everything would be all right, that everything I was going through was part of some plan and that the plan was perfect."

"Did he tell you that?"

"No, he didn't have to. In fact, he didn't say anything. I just felt these things, but somehow they seemed to be coming from him. I could feel everything. I knew everything. I knew there was nothing to fear . . . ever . . . and then he walked away."

"What else?"

"I felt very light. The last thing I remember is floating in the clouds. I was feeling so loved and so safe. . . . Then I woke up."

"How do you feel now?"

"I feel okay, but it's fading. I can remember everything about the dream, but the feeling is getting weaker. The traffic driving over here didn't help."

Everyday life, interfering again with transcendent experiences.

A woman wrote to me, thanking me for writing my first book. The information in the book helped her to understand and accept two dreams she had had—dreams that were more than two decades apart. Her letter was destroyed when Hurricane Andrew ripped through my office, but I remember it well.

From the time she was a young girl she knew that she would have a special child named David. She grew older, got married, and had two daughters but no son. She reached her midthirties, and she became more and more concerned. Where was David?

In a vivid dream an angel came to her and said, "You can have your son, but he can only stay for nineteen and a half years. Is that acceptable to you?"

The woman agreed.

A few months later, she became pregnant, and soon David was born. He was indeed a special child—kind, sensitive, and loving. "An old soul," she would say.

She never told David about her dream and the agreement with the angel. It came to pass that he died at nineteen and a half years of age due to a rare type of cancer of the brain. She felt guilty, anguished, grief-stricken, despondent. Why had she accepted the angel's offer? Was she somehow responsible for David's death?

In a vivid dream a month after David's death, the angel reappeared. This time David was with the angel, and David spoke to her. "Don't grieve so," he said. "I love you. I chose you. You did not choose me."

And she understood.

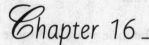

Chapter 16 _____

> *It is again a strong proof of men knowing most things before birth, that when mere children they grasp innumerable facts with such speed as to show that they are not then taking them in for the first time, but remembering and recalling them.*
>
> CICERO

I was momentarily confused. Pedro had walked through a door, in his mind, to another time and another place. By the movements of his eyes, I could tell that he was observing something. "You will be able to talk," I told him, "and yet you will be able to remain in a deep trance state and continue to observe and to experience. What do you see?"

"I see myself," Pedro answered. "I am lying in a field at night. The air is cool and clear. . . . I see many stars."

"Are you alone?"

"Yes. There's no one else around."

"What do you look like?" I asked, looking for details in order to learn more about the time and place in which he had emerged.

"I'm myself . . . about twelve years old. . . . My hair is short."

"You are yourself?" I questioned, still not realizing that Pedro had merely gone back into his own childhood and not a past life.

"Yes," he answered simply. "Back in Mexico as a boy."

Now I understood, and I shifted gears, looking more for feelings. I wanted to find out why his mind had selected this particular memory from the vast panorama available to it.

"How do you feel?"

"I feel very happy. There's something so peaceful about the night sky. The stars have always seemed so familiar and friendly to me. . . . I like to pick out the constellations and watch them march across the sky as the seasons change."

"Do you study the stars in school?"

"Not really, just a little bit. But I read about them on my own. Mostly I like to watch them."

"Does anyone else in your family enjoy watching the stars?"

"No," he answered, "only me."

I subtly shifted now to appeal to his higher self or intelligence, to his expanded perspective, to learn more about the importance of this memory. I was no longer speaking to the twelve-year-old Pedro.

"What is the importance of this memory of the night sky?" I asked. "Why did your mind select this particular one?"

He was silent for a while. His face softened in the thin afternoon light.

"The stars are a gift to me," he began softly. "They are a comfort. They are a symphony I have heard before, refreshing my soul, reminding me of what I had forgotten.

"They are even more," he continued, a bit enigmatically. "They are a path guiding me to my destiny . . . slowly but surely. . . . I must be patient and not get in the way. The schedule is already set." He was silent again.

I let him rest as a thought crept into my mind. The night sky has been here far longer than mankind. At some level, haven't we all heard that ancient symphony? Are all of our destinies guided as well? And then another thought, very clear in its words but not at all in its meaning. I, too, must be patient and not get in the way of Pedro's destiny.

This thought came to me like an instruction. It turned out to be a prophecy.

As patients like Elizabeth and Pedro challenged many of my old beliefs about life and death and even about psychotherapy, I also had begun to meditate, or at least to muse, every day. In deeply relaxed states, thoughts, images, and ideas often popped suddenly into my awareness.

One day a thought came with the urgency of a message. I needed to take a close look at those patients of mine who had been in therapy for a long period of time, my chronic patients. Somehow I would now see them more clearly, and this clarity of vision would also teach me more about myself.

Those patients who were coming to me now for regression therapy, visualization techniques, and spiritual counseling were doing extremely well. But what about this other population of patients, many of whom were in therapy with me before my books were published? Why would I see them more clearly now? What was I to learn about myself?

As it turned out, quite a lot. I had stopped being a teacher to many of these long-term patients; instead I had become a habit and a crutch. Many had become dependent on me, and instead of challenging them to be independent, I had accepted the old role.

I had become dependent on them, too. They paid the bills, flattered me, made me feel indispensable to them, and reinforced the stereotype of the physician as demigod in our society. I had to face my ego.

One by one I faced my fears. Security was the first. Money is neither good nor bad, and although important at times it confers no real security. I needed more faith. In order to take risks, to commit myself to right action, I had to know that I would be all right. I examined my values, what was important in my life and what was not. As I remembered and realigned my faith and values, my concerns about money and security disappeared, like a fog lifting in the sunlight. I felt very safe.

I looked at my indispensability and my need to feel important. This is another illusion of the ego. We are all spiritual beings, I remembered. All of us are equal beneath our exteriors. All of us are important.

My need to be special, to be loved, could only truly be met at a spiritual level, from deep within myself, from the divinity within. My family could help, but only up to a point. Certainly not my patients. I could teach them, and they could teach me. We could help each other for a while, but we could never satisfy each other's *deepest* needs. That quest is a spiritual one.

Physicians are highly trained teachers and healers but hardly demigods. We are just highly trained people. Physicians are spokes on the same wheel as all the other helpers in our society.

People often hide behind their professional labels and facades (doctor, lawyer, senator, and so on), most of which

were not even built before our twenties or thirties. We
have to remember who we were before our titles were
conferred.

It is not only that we are all capable of *becoming* loving
and spiritual people, people who are charitable, kind, and
peaceful, filled with serenity and joy. We already *are*. We
have just forgotten, and our egos seem to prevent us from
remembering.

Our vision is clouded. Our values are upside-down.

Many psychiatrists have talked to me about feeling
trapped by their patients. They have lost the joy of
helping.

I remind them that they are spiritual beings, too. They
are trapped by their insecurities and by their egos. They,
too, need the courage to take risks and to leap into health
and joy.

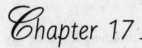

Chapter 17 _____

For we have come by different ways to this place. I have no feeling that we met before. No déjà vu. I don't think it was you in lavender by the sea as I rode by in A.D. 1206 or beside me in the border wars. Or there in the Gallatins, a hundred years ago, lying with me in the silver-green grass above some mountain town. I can tell by the natural ease with which you wear fine clothes and the way your mouth moves when you speak to waiters in good restaurants. You have come the way of castles and cathedrals, of elegance and empire.

ROBERT JAMES WALLER

By the time I had finished counting backward from ten to one, Elizabeth was already in a deep hypnotic trance. Her eyes were fluttering under their lids. Her body was limp, and her breathing had slowed into a very relaxed rhythm. Her mind was now ready for time travel.

I took her back slowly, this time using a peaceful mountain stream as a gateway to the distant past. She walked across the stream into a beautiful light. Walking through the light, she emerged in another time and another place, in an ancient lifetime.

"I'm wearing thin sandals," she observed, after I had instructed her to look at her feet. "There's a binding just above the ankles. I have a long white dress of different lengths. Over it is a veil-like covering down to my ankles. The sleeves are very wide and end at my elbows. I'm

119

wearing golden bracelets at three different levels of my arms." She was observing herself vividly and with great detail.

"My hair is dark brown and long, below my shoulders. . . . My eyes are brown, too. . . . My skin is light brown."

"You are a girl," I assumed.

"Yes," she patiently answered.

"About how old are you?"

"About fourteen."

"What do you do? Where do you live?" I fired at her, asking two questions before she had a chance to answer.

"On the temple grounds," she responded. "I'm training to be a healer and to help the priests."

"Do you know the name of this land?" I asked.

"It is Egypt . . . a long time ago."

"Do you know the year?"

"No," she replied. "I don't see that . . . but it is very long ago . . . very old."

I returned to her memories and experiences of that ancient time.

"How did you happen to receive this training, to be a healer and to work with the priests?"

"I was selected by the priests, just as the others were. We are all chosen, according to our talents and abilities. . . . The priests know this from the time we are very young."

I wanted to know more about this selection process.

"How do the priests know about your talents? Do they observe you in school or with your parents?"

"Oh, no," she corrected me. "They know intuitively. They are very wise. They know who has the ability in numbers and should be an engineer or a counter or a treasurer. They know who can write and scribe. They know who has military potential and should be trained to lead armies. They know who will make the best administrators. These will be trained to be governors and officials. They know those who possess healing and intuitive abilities, and these are trained to be healers and advisers and even to be priests."

"So the priests decide what occupations people train for," I summarized.

"Yes," she concurred. "Talents and potentials are divined by the priests when the child is very young. His training is then set. . . . He has no choice."

"Is this training open to everyone?"

"Oh, no," she objected. "Only to those of the nobility, to those related to the pharaoh."

"You must be related to the pharaoh?"

"Yes, but his family is very large. Even distant cousins are considered part of the family."

"But what of very talented people who are not related?" I asked, my curiosity causing me to linger at this family selection system.

"They can get some training," she again patiently explained. "But they can only progress so far . . . to be assistants to the leaders, who are relatives of the royal family."

"Are you a relative of the pharaoh?" I asked.

"A cousin . . . not too close."

"Close enough," I uttered.

"Yes," she answered.

I decided to move on, even though I already knew that the patient after Elizabeth had cancelled her appointment that day, so time was not hurrying me along as much as usual.

"Do you have any family with you?"

"Yes, my brother. We are very close. He is two years older. He has also been chosen to train as a healer and priest and we are together here. Our parents live some distance away, so it is very good to have my brother with me. . . . I can see him now."

I risked another distraction, looking for clues to understanding Elizabeth's relationships. "Look closely at his face. Look into his eyes. Do you recognize him as anybody in your current life?"

She seemed to be peering into his face. "No," she said sadly. "I don't recognize him."

I had somewhat expected her to recognize her beloved mother, or perhaps her brother or father. But there was no identification.

"Go ahead in time now to the next important event in that Egyptian girl's life. You can remember everything." She went forward in time.

"I am eighteen now. My brother and I are much more advanced now. He is wearing a white and gold skirt that is short. It ends just above his knees. . . . He is very handsome," she noted.

"How are you more advanced?" I inquired, bringing her focus back to the training.

"We have many more skills. We are working with special healing rods that, when mastered, greatly speed up the regeneration of tissues and limbs." She paused for a few moments, studying these rods.

"They contain a liquid energy that flows through the rods. . . . The energy is concentrated at the point of regeneration. . . . You can use this to grow limbs and heal tissue, even dying or dead tissue."

I was surprised. Even modern medicine cannot accomplish these feats, although nature can, as with salamanders and other lizards, which can regrow detached limbs or tails. The latest research in traumatic spinal cord injuries is just now leading to the beginning of controlled nerve regeneration, about four to five thousand years after Elizabeth's work with healing rods that could induce limb and tissue regeneration.

She could not articulate how the rods worked, other than with energy. Elizabeth did not have the vocabulary or mental concepts to understand and explain.

She began to speak again, and the reasons for her lack of understanding became clear.

"At least that's what they tell me. I am young and a girl. I have held the rods, but I have never seen them work. I have not yet seen the regeneration. . . . My brother has seen this. He is allowed, and when he is older he will be allowed this knowledge of regeneration. My training will be ended before that level. I cannot progress to that level, for I am a female," she explained.

"He will be allowed the knowledge of regeneration, and you will not?" I questioned.

"That is true," she commented. "He will be allowed to know higher secrets, but I will not."

She paused, then added, "I am not jealous of him. It is the custom . . . a foolish custom, because I have more ability to heal than many men."

Her voice dropped to a whisper.

"He will tell me the secrets anyway. . . . He has promised me. He will teach me how the rods work, too. He has already explained many things to me. . . . He has told me they are trying to revive people who have recently died!"

"Who have died?" I echoed.

"Yes, but this must be done very quickly," she added.

"How do they do this?"

"I don't know. . . . They use several of the rods. There are special chants. The body must be positioned in a certain way. There is more, but I do not know. . . . When my brother learns, he will tell me." She ended her explanation.

My logical mind arrived at the assumption that the people allegedly being revived were not really dead yet but probably *near* death, like patients recovering from near-death experiences. After all, they did not have equipment to monitor brainwave function in those days. They could not pinpoint the absence of brain activity, which is our modern definition of death.

My intuitive sense told me to keep an open mind. Other explanations could exist, explanations beyond my current comprehension.

Elizabeth was still silent, so I resumed the questioning.

"Are there other forms of healing that you do?" I asked her.

"There are many," she responded. "One is with our hands. We touch the area of the body that needs the healing and send energy directly there . . . through our hands. Some don't even need to touch the body. We feel above the person's body for areas of heat. We disperse the heat and smooth the energy. The heat must be dispersed at several levels above the body, not just the closest," she explained. She was speaking rapidly now, describing ancient variations of healing techniques.

"Others can heal mentally. They can see the problem areas in their minds, and they mentally send energy to those spots. I can't do this yet," she added, "but I will learn eventually.

"Some touch the person's pulse with their second and third fingers held together and send energy directly into the flow of blood. You can reach the internal organs this way, and you can see the cleansing energy leaving through the person's toes." Elizabeth continued her rapid and increasingly technical explanation.

"I am working now with putting people into very deep levels of trance and having them also see the healing as it occurs, so that they complete the healing transformation on the mental level. We give them potions to help them go very deep." She paused for a moment.

Except for the potions, this last technique very much resembles the hypnotic visualizations that I and others are using in the late twentieth century to stimulate the healing process.

"Are there more methods?" I inquired.

"The ones that evoke the gods are reserved for the priests," she answered. "These are forbidden to me."

"Forbidden?"

"Yes, because women cannot become priests. We can become healers, and we assist the priests, but we cannot do their functions. . . . Oh, some women call themselves priestesses and play musical instruments in the ceremonies, but they have no power." With some sarcasm in her voice, she added, "They are musicians like I am a healer; they are hardly priests. Even Hathor mocks them."

Hathor was the Egyptian goddess of love, mirth, and joy. She was also the goddess of festivity and dance. Elizabeth was probably remembering one of Hathor's more esoteric functions, that of defender and protectress of women. Hathor's mockery of these priestesses underlined the empty grandiosity of their titles.

Elizabeth grew silent again, and as she did, my mind

drew parallels to the current time. Glass ceilings seem to be as old as time itself.

The road to advancement in this period of primitive Egypt seemed to be restricted to only a few. Relatives of the pharaoh, who himself was considered half divine, could advance, but female relatives would soon bump into the gender barrier. Male relatives of the pharaoh were the privileged few.

Elizabeth was still silent, and I urged her forward. "Go ahead in time to the next important event in that life. What do you see?"

"My brother and I are advisers now," she commented, after progressing a few more years into the future. "We stand behind the governor of this area and we advise him. He is a great administrator and a good military leader, too. But he is impulsive and needs our intuition and inner guidance. . . . We help to balance him."

"Are you happy doing this?"

"Yes, it is good to be with my brother. . . . And the governor is usually kind. He often listens to our advice. . . . We do our healing work also." She seemed contented, if not ecstatic. She had not married, so her brother was her family. I moved her ahead in time.

She was visibly upset now. She began to cry, then stopped. "I know too much for this. I must be strong. It is not that I fear exile or death. Not at all. But to leave my brother . . . that is hard!" Another tear fell.

"What happened?" I asked, somewhat startled at the sudden decline in her fortunes.

"The governor's son became severely ill. He died before anything could be done. He knows about our work with regeneration and our attempts to bring the recently dead back to life. So he *demanded* that I bring his son back from the dead. If I did not, I would be sent to permanent exile. I know that place. Nobody returns."

"And the son?" I asked hesitantly.

"He could not be returned. It was not allowed. So I had to be punished." She was again sad and the tears welled up once more in her eyes.

"It makes no sense," she said slowly. "I was never allowed to learn about the rods. . . . I was never allowed to acquire the knowledge of regeneration and revival. My brother taught me a little, but not enough. . . . They didn't know he told me anything."

"What happened to your brother?"

"He was away, so he was spared. All the priests were away. Only I was around. . . . He returned in time to see me before the exile began. I don't fear exile or death, only leaving him. . . . There is no choice."

"How long are you in exile?" I asked.

"Not very long," she answered. "I know how to leave my body. One day I left my body and did not return. That was my death, for without the soul, the body dies." She had jumped to that point and was speaking from a higher perspective.

"As simple as that?"

"There is no pain, no interruption in awareness when such a death is chosen. That is why I did not fear death. I knew I could never see my brother again. I could not do my work on that barren island. There was no reason to stay in physical form. The gods understand."

She was silent, resting. I knew that her love for her brother would survive physical death, as would her brother's love for her. Love is eternal. Had they met again over the intervening centuries? Would they meet again in the future?

I also knew that this memory would help ease her grief. Once more she had found herself in the distant past. Her consciousness, her soul, had survived physical death and centuries of time to emerge once again, this time as Elizabeth. If she could survive through time, so could her mother. So could all of us. She had not found her mother in ancient Egypt, but she had found a beloved brother, a companion soul whom she could not recognize in her current life. At least not yet.

I like to think of soul relationships as similar to a large tree with a thousand leaves on it. Those leaves that are on your twig are intimately close to you. You may even share experiences, soul experiences, among yourselves. There may be three or four or five leaves on your twig. You are also highly and closely related to the leaves on the branch next to yours. They share a common limb. They are close to you, but not as close as the leaves on your own twig. Similarly, as you extend farther out along the tree, you are still related to these other leaves or souls, but not as closely as those in your immediate proximity. You are all part of one tree and one trunk. You can share experiences. You know each other. But those on your twig are the closest.

There are many other trees in this beautiful forest. Each tree is connected to the others through the root system in the ground. So even though there may be a leaf on a distant tree that seems quite different from you and very far away, you are still connected to that leaf. You are connected to all leaves. But you are the most closely connected to those on your tree. And even more intimately connected to those on your branch. And almost as one with those on your own twig.

You probably have met the other souls farther out on your tree in previous lifetimes. They may have been in many different relationships with you. Their interactions may have been extremely brief. Even a thirty-minute encounter could have helped you learn a lesson or helped them or the both of you, as is usually the case. One of these souls may have been the beggar in the road to whom you gave a heart's gift, allowing you to extend your compassion to another human being and allowing the recipient to learn about receiving love and help. You and the beggar may have never met again in that lifetime, and yet you are part of the drama. Your meetings vary in duration—five minutes, one hour, a day, a month, a decade, or more—this is how souls relate. Relationships are not measured in time but in lessons learned.

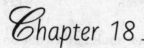

Chapter 18

> *How interesting it would be to write the story of the*
> *experiences in this life of a man who killed himself*
> *in his previous life; how he now stumbles against the*
> *very demands which had offered themselves before,*
> *until he arrives at the realization that he must fulfil*
> *those demands. . . . The deeds of the preceding life*
> *give direction to the present life.*
>
> TOLSTOY

*H*e felt the message sear itself into his soul. The living words pressed themselves forever into his being. As he rested after leaving his splattered body, we both pondered the different levels of meaning of these outwardly simple words.

The session had begun in the usual way. I regressed Pedro using a rapid induction, and he slipped quickly into a deeply tranquil state. His breathing became deep and even, and his muscles relaxed completely. His mind, focused by the hypnosis, penetrated the customary limits of space and time, and he remembered events that had happened far before his birth as Pedro.

"I'm wearing brown shoes," he observed as he emerged in the physical confines of a previous incarnation. "They're old and battered. . . . I'm a man around forty years old," he added without my prodding. "Balding on the top with hair beginning to gray. My sideburns and beard are gray already. My beard is short, and it's shaved pretty far down my cheeks."

He was paying considerable attention to minor details. I appreciated the accuracy of his description, but I was also aware of time slipping by.

"Go ahead," I advised. "Find out what you're doing in this life. Go to the next significant event."

"My glasses are small and wire-rimmed," he noted, still occupied with physical features. "My nose is wide, and my skin is very pale."

It is not unusual for a hypnotized patient to be resistant to my suggestions. I have learned that you can't always guide the patient; sometimes the patient has to guide you.

"What do you do in this life?" I asked.

"I'm a doctor," he answered quickly, "a country doctor. I work very hard. The people are mostly poor, but I get by. They are good people overall."

"Do you know the name of the place where you live?"

"I believe it is in this country, in Ohio. . . ."

"Do you know the year?"

"Late eighteen-hundreds, I think."

"And your name?" I delicately inquired.

"Thomas . . . my name is Thomas."

"Do you have a last name?"

"It starts with a D . . . Dixon or Diggins or something like that. . . . I don't feel well," he added.

"What's wrong?"

"I feel very sad . . . very sad. I don't want to go on living!" He had jumped ahead to a time of crisis.

"What is making you so sad?" I inquired.

"I have been despondent before," he clarified. "It comes and goes, but this is the worst. It's never been this bad before. The both things are just overwhelming. . . . I can't go on this way."

"What 'both things'?" I echoed.

"My patient died. The fever killed him. They trusted me to save him. They put their faith in me, and I couldn't. I've let them down. . . . Now they have no husband, no father. They will have to struggle to survive. . . . I couldn't save him!"

"Sometimes patients die despite our best efforts. Especially in the eighteen-hundreds," I added, paradoxically attempting to ease his guilt and despair over an event that had occurred a century ago. I could not alter the event, only his attitude toward it. I knew that Thomas had already experienced and acted upon his feelings. What was done was done. But I could still help Pedro, by helping him to understand, by helping him to see from a higher and more detached perspective.

He was silent. I hoped that I had not jarred him from that doctor's lifetime by doing therapy aimed at a level of understanding beyond Thomas. I had not even found out the other event that had precipitated his depression.

"What is the other thing causing your sadness?" I asked, trying to put the genie back into the bottle.

"My wife has left me," he answered. I was relieved to be talking to Thomas again.

"She has left you?" I repeated, encouraging him to elaborate.

"Yes," he answered sadly. "Our life was too difficult. We couldn't even have children. She went back to her family in Boston. . . . I'm very ashamed. . . . I couldn't help her. I couldn't make her happy."

I did not even attempt therapy with his higher mind at this time. Instead, I asked Thomas to move ahead in time to the next important event in that life. We could do the therapy later, as he reviewed this life while still in the hypnotized state, or even later, after he emerged from the hypnosis.

"I have a gun," he explained. "I'm going to shoot myself and end this misery!"

I suppressed the urge to ask him why he chose a gun and not one of the many medicines or poisons available to a doctor of that time. He had made his decision at least a century ago. The question itself was probably my way of intellectualizing his despair, despair of such magnitude as to drive him to self-annihilation.

"What happens next?" I asked instead.

"I've done it," he said simply. "I've shot myself in the mouth, and now I can see my body. . . . So much blood! So much blood!" He had already left his body and was seeing it at a distance.

"How do you feel now?" I asked.

"Confused. . . . I'm still sad. . . . I'm so tired," he answered. "But I can't rest. Not yet. . . . Someone is here for me."

"Who is there?"

"I don't know. Someone very important. He has something to tell me."

"What does he tell you?"

"That I have lived a good life, until the end. I should not have ended my life. Yet he seems to know I would do what I did."

"Is there more?" I asked, pushing this paradox aside. The answer came directly at me now, in a more powerful voice. Was this Thomas, or Pedro, or someone else? I flashed back momentarily to the Masters who spoke through Catherine. Except this was years later, and Catherine was not here.

"It is the reaching out with love to help another that is important, not the results. Reach out with love. That is all you need to do. Love one another. The results of reaching out with love are not the results you look for. Results to the physical body. You must heal the hearts of men."

Both physicians, Thomas and I, were being addressed, and we both listened raptly as the message continued. The voice was more powerful, more sure, more didactic than Pedro's.

"I will teach you how to heal the hearts of men. You will understand. *Love one another!*"

We could both feel the force of these words as they were impressed into our being. The words were alive. We could never forget them.

Later, Pedro told me that he vividly saw and heard everything that this luminous visitor communicated— words that danced with light as they bridged the space between them.

I had heard the same words. I was sure they were also meant for me. Important lessons leapt at me. Reach out with love and compassion, and do not worry so much about outcomes. Do not attempt to end your life before its natural time. A higher wisdom deals with outcomes and knows the time for all things. Free will and destiny coexist. Do not measure healing by physical results. Healing occurs at many levels, not just the physical, and real healing must occur at the heart level. Somehow I would learn about healing the hearts of men. Most of all: Love one another. Timeless wisdom, easily grasped but practiced by only a few.

My mind drifted back to Pedro. Themes of separation and loss plagued his lifetimes. This time they had led him to suicide. He had been warned about not ending a life prematurely. But losses were occurring anew, and grief had returned. Would he remember or would hopeless despair overtake him once again?

How devastating it is to be a healer who cannot heal his patient. Elizabeth's "failure" in ancient Egypt. Pedro's despair as Thomas, the Ohio physician. My own painful experiences as a healer.

My first frustration as a healer who could not stop the onslaught of a rampaging illness occurred more than twenty-five years ago during my very first clinical rotation as a third-year student at Yale Medical School. I began with pediatrics, and I was assigned to Danny, a seven-year-old boy with a large Wilms' tumor. This is a malignant tumor of the kidney that occurs almost exclusively in childhood. The younger the child, the better the prognosis. Seven was not considered young for this cancer.

Danny was the first real patient in my medical career. Prior to him, all of my experience had been in classrooms, lecture halls, laboratories, and sitting for endless hours in front of my textbooks. The third year began our clinical experience. We were assigned to hospital wards with real patients. Enough facts and theory. The time for practical application had arrived.

I had to draw Danny's blood for the laboratory tests, and I took care of all the minor procedures, called "scut work" by more advanced practitioners but very meaningful to third-year medical students.

Danny was a wonderful child, but our bond was even stronger and more special because he was my first patient.

Danny fought heroically. He had lost his hair from the powerful but toxic chemotherapy treatments. His belly was severely bloated. Yet he was rallying, and his parents and I took hope. A good percentage of children were able to recover from this type of malignancy at that time.

I was the youngest member of the treatment team. The medical student usually knew less clinical medicine than the intern, resident, or attending physician, all of whom were incredibly busy with their work. On the other hand, the medical student had more time to spend with the patient and family. In general, the medical student also placed a higher priority on getting to know the patient and his family. We would customarily be assigned to talk to the family or to convey messages to the patient.

Danny was my main patient, and I liked him a lot. I spent many hours sitting on the side of his bed, playing games, reading stories, or just talking. I admired his courage. I also spent time with his parents, frequently in Danny's dark and drab hospital room. We even ate together in the cafeteria. They were frightened but also encouraged by his rally.

Suddenly, Danny took a drastic turn for the worse. A dangerous respiratory infection overwhelmed his weakened immune system. He had difficulty breathing, and his usually bright eyes turned dull and glazed. I was shunted aside by the more senior members of the medical team. Antibiotics were started and stopped and changed, to no avail. Danny slid downhill. I stayed with his mother and father, feeling helpless and horrified. The illness won. Danny died.

I was too upset to spend more time with his parents, beyond a brief word and a hug. I identified with their pain as much as I could at that time. Three years later, when my own son died in a hospital, I understood even more. But at the time, I felt some vague responsibility for his death, as if I should have done something, anything, to avert it.

The "failure" to heal strikes at the very soul of every healer. I understood Thomas's despair.

Far fewer psychiatric patients die of their illnesses. Yet the inability to help a severely disturbed patient evokes chords of the same frustration and sense of helplessness.

When I was chairman of the Psychiatry Department at Mount Sinai, I treated a beautiful and talented woman in her thirties. A successful career woman, she had recently entered into a happy marriage. Gradually she became paranoid, and the paranoia was worsening despite medicines, despite therapy, despite every intervention. Neither I nor any consultant I called in could determine why, because her course and symptoms and tests were very atypical for schizophrenia, mania, or any other of the usual psychoses. She had begun to deteriorate soon after a trip to the Far East, and one test showed extremely high antibodies to a parasite. Still, no medical or psychiatric treatment helped, and she gradually worsened.

Again, I had felt the pangs of helplessness, the frustration of the healer who could not heal.

To reach out with love, to do your best and not be so concerned with results or outcomes, that is the answer. This simple concept, ringing so true to me, is the balm of understanding that healers need. In a sense, I had reached out with love to Danny, and he had reached back to me.

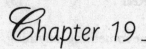

Chapter 19

Elizabeth was frustrated and despondent. Her new relationship had lasted for only two dates. Bob was avoiding her. She had known him casually for more than a year, through work. He was successful and handsome and shared many of her interests. He told her that his long-term affair with a married woman had just ended. Bob had had several short-term relationships with other women, but there always seemed to be something lacking in these women. According to him, they would turn out to be superficial or unintelligent or not share his values, and he would end the relationships. His married lover would always accept him back. Her husband was rich, but their relationship lacked passion. She would not leave her husband and their affluent life.

"You're different from the others," Bob swore to Elizabeth. "We have so much more in common." He told Elizabeth that she was more intelligent than any of the others, more beautiful, that he knew their relationship could last.

Elizabeth convinced herself that Bob was right. "He was there all the time, and I never really noticed," she thought. "Sometimes the answer is right in front of your eyes and you never see it."

She forgot that the reason she never really noticed Bob and his blond good looks was that she never felt a chemistry with him. She was lonely and desperate for a man's arms. She listened to her head and ignored her heart's warning.

Their first date was very promising. They went out for a casual dinner, a good movie, and intimate conversation while watching the wind-whipped waves on the beach under the cool light of a nearly full moon. "I could fall in love with you," he told her, teasing her with a promise that would never be fulfilled. Her head carefully heard every word, ignoring the lack of response from her heart.

The second date seemed fine. She had a good time, and she sensed that he did, too. His affection seemed genuine, and he hinted at sex in the future. But he never called back.

Finally she called him. He said that he wanted to see her again but that he was very busy, and it was difficult to pick an exact time. He assured her he had not had a change of heart. He *did* want to see her; he just couldn't tell her when.

"Why do I always pick losers?" she asked me. "What's wrong with me?"

"You don't pick losers," I told her. "Here's a handsome and successful man who told you he was interested and available. Don't blame yourself."

I didn't say so, but inwardly I knew she was right. She *was* picking losers, in this case an emotional loser. It turned out he could not leave the safety of his married lover. He chose to remain dependent and "safe." Elizabeth became the victim of his fear and his lack of courage. Better now than later, I thought. Elizabeth was strong; she would recover.

Elizabeth asked if we still had time to attempt a regression. She could sense something important was near the surface, and she was anxious to find it, so we proceeded.

After she emerged in an ancient past life, I was not sure we had made the right decision.

She saw a land of broad, rolling plains and flat-topped hills. A land of yaklike animals and small agile horses, of large rounded tents and nomadic wanderers. It was a land of passion, and it was a land of violence.

Her husband was away with most of the other men, hunting or raiding. The enemy struck, flying in on waves of horses against the depleted defenders. Her husband's parents were killed first, hacked down by broad, razor-sharp swords. Her baby was killed next, gutted by a spear. A shudder convulsed her spirit. She wanted to die, too, but such was not her destiny. Captured by the young warriors because of her beauty, she became the property of the strongest of the invading horde. A few other young women were also spared.

"Let me die!" she pleaded to her captor, but he would not allow it.

"You are mine now," he said simply. "You will live in my tent, and you will be my wife."

Except for her husband, whom she would never see again, all her loved ones were dead. She had no choice. She attempted to escape several times, only to be quickly caught. Her suicide attempts were similarly thwarted.

She hardened herself, and her depression turned into a constant smoldering anger, devouring her capacity to love. Her spirit withered, and she merely existed, a hardened heart trapped in a living body. No jail could be as confining or as cruel.

"Let's go back in time," I suggested. "Let's go back before your village was raided." I counted back from three to one.

"What do you see?" I asked.

Her face was now serene and peaceful as she remembered the early years, growing up, laughing and playing with the man she would eventually marry. She loved this childhood friend dearly, and he returned this love to her. She was at peace.

"Do you recognize this man you married? Look into his eyes."

"No, I don't," she finally answered.

"Look at the others in your village. Do you recognize anyone?"

She looked carefully at her relatives and friends in that lifetime.

"Yes . . . yes, my mother is there!" Elizabeth gasped happily. "She is the mother of my husband. We are very close. When my own mother died, she took me in as a daughter. I recognize her!"

"Do you recognize anyone else?" I inquired.

"She lives in the largest tent, with the flags and white feathers," she answered, ignoring my question.

Her face darkened.

"They killed her, too!" she lamented, jumping back to the massacre.

"Who killed her? Where did they come from?"

"From the east, from beyond the wall. . . . This is where they have taken me."

"Do you know the name of their land?"

She pondered this question. "No. It seems to be somewhere in Asia, in the northern part. Maybe the west of China. . . . We have oriental features."

"It's okay," I responded. "Let's move ahead in time within that lifetime. What happens to you?"

"I was finally allowed to kill myself, after I had grown older and was not so attractive anymore," she answered, without much emotion. "I think they grew tired of me," she added.

She was floating now, having left her body.

I asked her to review her life. "What do you see? What were the lessons? What did you learn?"

Elizabeth was silent for a few moments. And then she answered, "I learned many things. I learned of anger and the foolishness of holding on to anger. I could have worked with the younger children, with the old ones, with the sick ones, in the enemy's town. I could have taught them. . . . I could have loved them . . . but I never allowed myself to love. I never allowed myself to let my anger dissipate. I never allowed myself to open my heart once again. And these children, at least, were innocent. They were souls entering into this world. They had nothing to do with the raid, with the deaths of my loved ones.

And yet I blamed them, too. I carried the anger even to
the new generations, and this is foolish. It could hurt
them, but most of all it harmed me. . . . I never permitted
myself to love again." She paused. "And I had much love
to give."

She paused again and then seemed to speak from an
even higher source.

"Love is like a fluid," she began. "It fills up crevices.
It fills empty spaces of its own accord. It is we, it is people
who stop it by erecting false barriers. And when love
cannot fill our hearts and our minds, when we are discon-
nected from our souls, which consist of love, then we all
go crazy."

I considered her words. I knew that love was important,
perhaps even the most important thing in the world. But
it had never dawned on me that the absence of love could
cause us to lose our minds.

I remembered the famous monkey experiments of the
psychologist, Dr. Harry Harlow, in which young monkeys
deprived of touching, of nurturing, of love became completely asocial, physically ill, or even died. They could
not survive intact without it. Loving is not an option. It
is a necessity.

I turned back to Elizabeth. "Look ahead in time. How
does what you learned then affect you now? And how
can this learning, how can this remembering, help you
in your current life to feel happier, more peaceful, more
loving?"

"I must learn to let go of anger, to not hold it in, to
recognize it, recognize its roots and let it go. I must feel
free to love, to not hold back, and yet I still search. I
haven't found someone to love completely, uncondition-
ally. There always seems to be a problem."

She fell silent for half a minute. Suddenly she was speaking with a voice much deeper and slower than usual. The room felt very cold.

"God is one," she began. She struggled for words. "It is all one vibration, one energy. The only difference is the rate of vibration. So God and people and rocks have the same relationship as steam and water and ice. Everything, all that is, is made up of the one. Love breaks down the barriers and creates unity. That which creates barriers and creates separateness and differences is ignorance. You must teach them these things."

That was the end of the message. Elizabeth was resting.

I thought of Catherine's messages, which seemed so similar to Elizabeth's. Even the room felt cold when Catherine would relay these messages, much as the room felt cold with Elizabeth. I pondered her words. Healing is the act of bringing together, removing the barriers. Separation is what causes harm. Why is it so difficult for people to grasp this concept?

Although I have conducted more than a thousand individual past-life regressions with my patients and many more in groups, I have had only a half dozen of these experiences myself. I have had some remembrances in vivid dreams and during a shiatsu, or acupressure, treatment. Some of these are described in my earlier books.

When my wife, Carole, finished a course in hypnotherapy to add to her skills as a social worker, she conducted a few past-life regression sessions with me as the patient. I wanted to experience this with someone whom I trusted and who was well trained.

I had been practicing meditation for years, and I went under deeply and quickly. When the memories started to flood into my mind, they were primarily visual and quite vivid, like my dream images.

I could see myself as a young man from a wealthy Jewish family in Alexandria, around the time of Christ. Our community, I somehow knew, helped to finance the huge golden doors of the Great Temple in Jerusalem. My studies included Greek and the philosophy of the ancient Greeks, especially the followers of Plato and Aristotle.

I remembered one fragment of my life as that young man, when I attempted to augment my classical education by traveling among the clandestine desert communities in the southern deserts and caves of Palestine and the north of Egypt. Each community was a type of learning center, usually of mystical and esoteric knowledge. Some of these probably were Essene villages.

I traveled very simply, carrying only a little food and some clothes. Just about everything I needed was provided for me along the way. My family had money, and we were known to these peoples.

The spiritual knowledge I was acquiring was exciting and accelerated, and I enjoyed the journey.

For several weeks along the way from community to community, I was joined by a man about my age. He was taller than I and had intense brown eyes. We both wore robes and had cloths on our heads. He emanated peace, and as we studied together with the wise men of the villages, he soaked up the teachings much more quickly than I. Afterward, he would teach me as we camped together by desert fires.

After a few weeks, we separated. I went to study at a small synagogue near the Great Pyramid, and he went to the west.

Many of my patients, including Elizabeth and Pedro, have remembered lives in the area of ancient Palestine. Many have remembered Egypt.

For me, as for them, the images seemed extremely vivid and quite real.

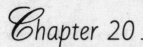

Chapter 20

O youth or young man, who fancy that you are neglected by the Gods, know that if you become worse you shall go to the worse souls, or if better to the better, and in every succession of life and death you will do and suffer what like may fitly suffer at the hands of like. This is the justice of heaven.

PLATO

Sometimes life's most significant events are upon you before you are aware of them, like the silent approach of a jungle cat. How could you not have noticed something of such magnitude? The camouflage is psychological.

Denial, the act of not seeing what is right before your eyes, because you really don't want to see, is the greatest disguise. Add in fatigue, distractions, rationalizations, mental escape, and all the other businesses of the mind that get in the way. Fortunately destiny's persistence can pierce the disguises and distinguish that which you need to see, the foreground emerging from the background, like mastering one of those magic-eye pictures.

Over the past fifteen years, I have often treated couples or families who have discovered each other together in past lives. Sometimes I have regressed couples who simultaneously and for the first time have found themselves interacting in the same prior lifetime. These revelations are often shocking to the couple. They have not experienced

147

anything like this before. They are silent while the scenes
are unfolding in my psychiatric office. It is only afterward,
after emerging from the relaxed, hypnotic state, that they
first discover they have been watching the same scenes,
feeling the same emotions. It is only then that I also
become aware of their past connections.

But with Elizabeth and Pedro, everything was backward. Their lives, and their lifetimes, were unfolding
independently and quite separately, in my office. They
did not know each other. They had never met. They
were from different countries and cultures. They came
to the office on different days. Seeing them both separately
and never even suspecting a link between them, I did
not make the connection. They had loved each other and
lost each other across lifetimes.

Why didn't I see it before? Was it even my destiny?
Am I supposed to be some cosmic matchmaker? Was I
distracted, fatigued, in denial? Was I rationalizing away
"coincidences"? Or was I right on schedule, the idea
dawning at its sunrise, the way it was planned all along.

It came to me one evening. "Eli?" I had heard it from
Elizabeth, weeks before, in my office.

Earlier that day, Pedro could not remember his name.
In a hypnotic trance, he had emerged in an ancient lifetime, one he had previously remembered in the office.
In that lifetime, he had died after being dragged by leather-
clad soldiers. His life ebbed away as his head rested in his
beloved daughter's lap, and she rocked rhythmically with
despair.

Perhaps there was more to learn from that time. Once
again, he remembered dying in her arms, his life fading
away. I asked him to look at her closely, to look deeply

into her eyes and to see if he recognized her as someone in his current life.

"No," he sadly answered. "I don't know her."

"Do you know your name?" I asked, returning his attention completely to that ancient lifetime in Palestine.

He pondered this question. "No," he finally said.

"I will tap you on the forehead as I count backward from three to one. Let your name just pop into your mind, into your awareness. Whatever name comes to you is fine."

No name popped into his mind.

"I don't know my name. Nothing comes to me!"

But something came to me, popping into my mind like a silent explosion, suddenly clear and vivid.

"Eli," I said aloud. "Is your name Eli?"

"How do you know that?" he responded from the ancient depths. "That *is* my name. Some call me Elihu, and some call me Eli. . . . How do you know? Were you there, too?"

"I don't know," I answered truthfully. "It just came to me."

I was very surprised at the whole situation. How *did* I know? I have had psychic or intuitive flashes before, but not often. This felt as if I were *remembering* something rather than receiving a psychic message. Remembering from when? I could not place it. My mind stretched to remember, but I could not.

I knew from experience that I should stop trying to remember. Let it go, get on with the day, the answer would probably arrive spontaneously in a while.

An important piece of some strange puzzle was missing. I could feel its absence, hinting at a crucial connection still to be found. But a connection to what? I tried, not very successfully, to concentrate on other things.

Later that evening, the puzzle piece arrived suddenly and very softly in my mind. All at once, I was aware of it.

It was Elizabeth. About two months ago, she had recounted a tragic but touching lifetime as a potter's daughter in ancient Palestine. Her father had been killed "accidentally" by Roman soldiers after they dragged him around from the back of a horse. The soldiers had not really cared what happened to him. His mangled body, his bleeding head, had been cradled by his daughter as he died in the dusty street.

She had remembered his name in that lifetime. His name was Eli.

My mind was working quickly now. The details of the two Palestinian lifetimes fit together. Pedro's and Elizabeth's memories of that time meshed perfectly. Physical descriptions, events, and names were the same. Father and daughter.

I have worked with many people, usually couples, who have found themselves together in previous lives. Many have recognized their soul companions, traveling together through time to be united once again in the current lifetime.

Never before had I encountered soulmates who had not yet met in the present time. In this case, soulmates who had traveled nearly two thousand years to be together again. They had come all this way. They were within inches and minutes of each other, but they had not yet connected.

At home, with their charts filed away in my office, I tried to remember if they had shared other lifetimes. No, not as monks. One story but not two, at least not yet. Not on the India trading routes, not in the mangrove swamps of Florida, not in the malarial Spanish Americas, not so far in Ireland. These were the only lifetimes I could remember.

Another thought dawned. Perhaps they *had* been together in some or all of those times but had not recognized each other, because they had not met in the present. There was no face, no name, no landmark in the present life, no one to connect to the people in previous incarnations.

Then I remembered Elizabeth's western China, the timeworn sweeping plains where her people were massacred and where she and a few other young women were captured. On these same plains, which Pedro pinpointed as Mongolia, he had returned to find his family, his kin, his people destroyed.

Pedro and I had assumed that his young wife had been killed amid the chaos, destruction, and despair described in his recall. She had not. She had been captured and taken away for the rest of a lifetime, never to be held again in the strong arms of her Mongol husband.

Now those arms had returned through the hazardous mists of time to hold her again, to hug her sweetly to his breast. But they did not know. Only I knew.

Father and daughter. Childhood lovers. Husband and wife. How many more times throughout history had they shared their lives and their love?

They were together again, but they didn't know it. Both were lonely, both suffering in their way. Both were starving, and yet a feast had been set before them, a feast they could not yet smell or taste.

I was severely constrained by the "laws" of psychiatry,

if not the more subtle rules of karma. The strictest of the laws is that of privacy or confidentiality. If psychiatry were a religion, breaching a patient's confidentiality would be one of its cardinal sins. At the least the breach could constitute malpractice. I could not tell Pedro about Elizabeth, nor Elizabeth about Pedro. Whatever the karma or spiritual consequences of intervening in another's free will, the consequences of violating psychiatry's main law were quite clear.

The spiritual consequences would not have deterred me. I could introduce them and let destiny take its course. The psychiatric consequences stopped me cold.

What if I were wrong? What if a relationship between them began, soured, and ended badly? There could be anger and bitterness. How would this reflect back on their feelings about me as their trusted therapist? Would their clinical improvement unravel? Would all their good therapeutic work be undone? There were definite risks.

I also had to examine my own subconscious motives. Was my need to see my patients become happier and healthier, to find peace and love in their lives, affecting my judgment now? Were my own needs urging me to cross the boundary of psychiatric ethics?

The easy choice would be to leave well enough alone, to say nothing. No harm done, no consequences. When in doubt, do no harm.

Whether or not to write *Many Lives, Many Masters* was a similar and very difficult decision. Writing my first book endangered my entire professional career. After four years of hesitation, I had decided to write it.

Once again, I chose to take the risk. I would intervene. I would try to nudge destiny along. As a concession to my training and to my fears, I would do it as carefully and as subtly as possible.

The scenes and details of specific historical epochs remembered by Elizabeth, Pedro, and many of my other patients are very similar to each other. These images are not necessarily like the ones we learned in Sunday school, from history books, or from television.

They are similar because they come from actual memories. Carolina Gomez, the former Miss Colombia and first runner-up in the 1994 Miss Universe pageant, remembered in one regression being a naked man pulled to his death by Roman horses. This death is similar to one remembered by Pedro. A few other patients have also remembered horse-drawn deaths, not only in Roman times but, unfortunately, in many other cultures as well.

A patient of mine from Colorado remembered being stolen from her Native American tribe and never seeing her family again. She eventually escaped, but she died in the equivalent of a mental ward in the Old West. How similar this is to Elizabeth's experience in Asia.

The theme of separation and loss is a common one in past-life regressions. We are all seeking to heal our psychic wounds. This need to heal emphasizes the remembering of old traumas, which have caused our pain and symptoms, rather than the remembering of serene and peaceful times, which have not left scars.

I occasionally work with two or more people at the same time. When I do this, I do not have either of them speak because they might disturb each other. Recently in my office I regressed a couple simultaneously. Their silent regression took up the entire session, and we had no time to review their experiences.

The couple left the office and began to compare notes. Incredibly, they had both experienced a lifetime together. In his lifetime he was a British officer in the thirteen colonies, and in hers she was a woman who lived there. They met and fell deeply in love. He was recalled to England and never again returned to visit his love. She was devastated by the loss, and yet there was nothing either one could do about it. Colonial society and the British military followed strict rules and customs.

They both saw and described the colonial woman in the same antique clothes. They both described the ship on which he had left the colonies to return to England and the tearful, sad parting that occurred at that time. All the details of their recall matched.

Their memories also illustrated problems in their current life relationship. One major problem was her nearly obsessive fear of separation from him and his constant need in return to reassure her that he was not going to leave her. Her fear and his need had no basis in the reality of their current relationship. The pattern had its roots in colonial times.

Other therapists performing past-life regressions are finding the same results. Traumas arise more frequently than peaceful memories. Death scenes are important because they are often traumatic. Lifetimes seem familiar and important scenes seem similar because the same themes and the same inventions of man have arisen at all times in all cultures.

"The thing that hath been, it is that which shall be; and that which is done is that which shall be done: and there is no new thing under the sun" (Ecclesiastes 1:9).

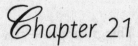

Chapter 21

Believing as I do in the theory of rebirth, I live in
the hope that if not in this birth, in some other birth
I shall be able to hug all humanity in friendly embrace.

MOHANDAS K. GANDHI

I was wrestling with time, and it had me in a bear hug.
Pedro was about to finish his therapy and move perma-
nently to Mexico. If Pedro and Elizabeth did not meet
soon, they would be in different countries, and the likelihood of their meeting in this lifetime would be dramatically diminished. Both of their grief reactions were
resolving. Physical symptoms, such as quality of sleep,
energy levels, and appetite, were better in both patients.

Their loneliness and their despair of finding a good
and loving relationship remained intact.

Anticipating Pedro's termination of therapy, I had
reduced the frequency of his appointments to every other
week. I did not have much time left.

I arranged for their next visits to be sequential, for
Pedro to follow Elizabeth in the hourly schedule that
day. Everybody entering or leaving my office has to pass
through the waiting room.

During Elizabeth's session, I worried that Pedro might

not come in for his appointment. Things happen—cars break down, emergencies arise, illnesses develop—and appointments are changed.

He appeared. I walked into the waiting room with Elizabeth. They looked at each other, and their eyes lingered for longer than a moment. I could sense the sudden interest, the hint at worlds of possibilities lying under the surface. Or was this just wishful thinking on my part?

Elizabeth's mind quickly reasserted its customary mastery, telling her she needed to leave, cautioning her about appropriate behavior. She turned to the outside door and left the offices.

I nodded to Pedro, and we walked into my office.

"A very attractive woman," he commented, as he sat down heavily in the large leather chair.

"Yes," I answered eagerly. "She's a very interesting person, too."

"That's nice," he said wistfully. His attention had already begun to wander. He turned to the task of terminating our sessions and moving on to the next phase of his life. He had pushed the brief meeting with Elizabeth out of his mind.

Neither Pedro nor Elizabeth followed up on this encounter in the waiting room. Neither asked for more information about the other. My manipulation had been too subtle, too fleeting.

I decided to try the back-to-back appointments again, two weeks later. Unless I chose to become more direct and to breach confidentiality by speaking directly to one or both of them, this would be my last chance. It was Pedro's final appointment prior to his move.

They gazed at each other again as I escorted her to the waiting room. Their eyes met and lingered even longer this time. Pedro nodded and smiled. Elizabeth smiled in return. She hesitated for a moment then turned to the door and left.

Trust yourself! I thought, trying to mentally remind Elizabeth of an important lesson. She did not respond.

Again, Pedro did not follow up. He did not ask me about Elizabeth. He was absorbed by the details of his relocation to Mexico, and he ended his therapy on that day.

Perhaps this is not to be, I thought. They were both improved, although not happy. Perhaps this was enough.

You will not always marry your most strongly bonded soulmate. There may be more than one for you, because soul families travel together. You might choose to marry a less bonded soul companion, one who has something specific to teach you or to learn from you. Your recognition of a soulmate may occur later in life, after both of you are already committed to your present-life families. Or your strongest soulmate connection may be to your parent, or to your child, or to your sibling. Or your strongest connection may be to a soulmate who has not incarnated during your lifetime and who is watching over you from the other side, like a guardian angel.

Sometimes your soulmate *is* willing and available. He or she might recognize the passion and the chemistry between you, the intimate and subtle bonds that imply connections over many lifetimes. Yet he or she may be toxic for you. It is a matter of soul development.

If one soul is less developed and more ignorant than the other, traits of violence, greed, jealousy, hatred, and fear might be brought into the relationship. These tendencies are toxic to the more evolved soul, even if from a soulmate. Frequently rescue fantasies arise with the thought, I can change him; I can help her grow. If he does not allow your help, if in her free will she chooses not to learn, not to grow, the relationship is doomed. Perhaps there will be another chance in another lifetime, unless he awakens later in this one. Late awakenings do happen.

Sometimes soulmates decide not to get married while incarnated. They arrange to meet, to stay together until the agreed upon task is completed, and then to move on. Their agendas, their lesson plans for the entirety of this life, are different, and they do not want to or need to spend all of this lifetime together. This is not a tragedy, only a matter of learning. You have eternal life together, but sometimes you may need to take separate classes.

A soulmate who is available but unawakened is a tragic figure and can cause you great anguish. Unawakened means that he or she does not see life clearly, is not aware of the many levels of existence. Unawakened means not knowing about souls. Usually it is the everyday mind that prevents awakening.

We hear the excuses of the mind all the time: I'm too young; I need more experience; I'm not ready to settle down yet; you are of a different religion (or race, region, social status, intellectual level, cultural background, and so on). These are all excuses, for souls possess none of these attributes.

The person may recognize the chemistry. The attraction is definitely there, but the source of the chemistry is not understood. It is delusional to believe that this passion, this soul recognition and attraction, will be easily found again with another person. You do not run into such a soulmate every day, perhaps only one or two more in a lifetime. Divine grace may reward a good heart, a loving soul.

Never worry about meeting soulmates. Such meetings are a matter of destiny. They *will* occur. After the meeting, the free will of both partners reigns. What decisions are made or not made are a matter of free will, of choice. The less awakened will make decisions based on the mind and all of its fears and prejudices. Unfortunately, this often leads to heartache. The more awakened the couple is, the more the likelihood of a decision based on love. When both partners are awakened, ecstasy is within their grasp.

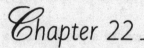

Chapter 22 _____

Read me, O Reader, if you find delight in me,
because very seldom shall I come back into this world.

LEONARDO DA VINCI

$\mathscr{F}$ortunately minds more creative than mine were expertly conspiring from lofty heights to arrange a meeting between Elizabeth and Pedro. The reunion was predestined. What happened afterward would be up to them.

Pedro was going to New York on business. After a few days there he was to leave for London for two weeks of business and vacation before returning to Mexico. Elizabeth was going to Boston for a business meeting and then a visit with her college roommate. They would be traveling on the same airline carrier but at different times.

When she reached the gate at the airport, Elizabeth found that her plane to Boston had been cancelled. Mechanical difficulties, she was told. Destiny was at work.

She was upset. She would have to call her friend and change the plans. The airline could get her to Newark, and she could catch the shuttle to Boston very early the next morning. She had an important business meeting in the morning which could not be missed.

Unbeknownst to her, these new arrangements put her on the same flight as Pedro. He was already there waiting for the flight to be called when she approached the gate. Catching her out of the corner of his eye, he carefully watched her check in at the counter and then take a seat in the waiting lounge. She occupied his attention entirely. He recognized her from their brief encounters in my waiting room.

A feeling of familiarity, of interest, overwhelmed him. His concentration was riveted on her as she opened a book. He watched her hair, her hands, how she sat and moved, and she seemed so familiar to him. He had seen her momentarily in the waiting room, but why *this* level of familiarity? They must have met before the time in the office. He racked his brain to find the hidden memory of where.

She felt herself being watched, but this often happened to her. She tried to concentrate on her reading. Concentration was difficult after all the hastily changed plans, but the meditation training had helped. She was able to clear her mind and focus on her book.

The feeling of being watched persisted. She looked up and saw him staring at her. She frowned, then smiled when she recognized him from their fleeting encounters in the waiting room. Instinctively she knew this man was safe. But how could she know that?

She looked at him for a moment more and then glanced back at her book, now completely unable to concentrate on the pages. Her heart began to beat more quickly, and her breathing accelerated. She *knew*, beyond any doubt, that he was being pulled by her, that very soon he would approach her.

She could feel him coming near. He introduced himself, and they began to talk. The attraction was mutual, immediate, and very strong. Within a few minutes he suggested that they change their seats so that they could sit together.

They were more than acquaintances before the airplane left the ground. Pedro seemed so familiar to her. She clearly knew how he would move, what he would say. Elizabeth had been very psychic when she was a child. The values and beliefs of her conservative midwestern upbringing had driven her intuitive talent underground, but all of her antennae were up now and at full attention.

Pedro could not take his eyes away from her face. He had never been so captivated with someone's eyes before. Hers had such clarity and such depth. Sky blue with a dark blue ring circling them, little hazel islands floating in the blue sea that engulfed him.

In his mind, he once again heard the words of the anguished woman wearing the white dress, the woman who had appeared in his recurrent dream.

"Hold her hand . . . reach out to her."

He hesitated. He wanted to hold her hand. Not yet, he thought. I hardly know her.

Somewhere near Orlando, thunderstorms began to rock the airplane as it plowed through the night sky. The sudden turbulence frightened her, and a brief expression of anxiety swept across her face.

Pedro noticed it instantly and his hand grasped hers, to comfort her. He knew it would.

The electricity touched his heart in the flash of a moment.

Elizabeth could feel lifetimes being awakened by the current.

The connection had been made.

★ ★ ★

Listen to your heart, to your own intuitive wisdom, when making important decisions, especially when deciding about a gift of destiny, such as a soulmate. Destiny will deposit its gift directly at your feet, but what you subsequently decide to do with that gift is up to you. If you rely exclusively on the advice of others, you may make terrible mistakes. Your heart knows what you need. Other people have other agendas.

My father, meaning well but partially blinded because of his own fears, objected to my plans to marry Carole. As I look back, Carole was one of destiny's wonderful gifts, a soul companion across the centuries, appearing again like a beautiful rose, blooming in its season.

Our problem was our youth. We met when I was only eighteen, having just finished my freshman year at Columbia. Carole was seventeen, about to begin college. Within a few months we knew we wanted to be together always. I had no desire to see anyone else, despite warnings from family that we were too young, that I did not have enough experience to make such a critical life decision. They did not understand that my heart had the experience of uncounted centuries, that it was certain beyond any rational comprehension. It was inconceivable that we would not be together.

My father's agenda became clear. If Carole and I married and had a child, I might have to leave school, and my hopes of becoming a physician would be dashed. In fact, this had happened to my father. He had been a pre-medical student at Brooklyn College during World War II, but my birth had forced him to work after he left military service. He never returned to medical school, and his dreams of becoming a physician never materialized. These dreams remained a bitterly unfulfilled potential, hovering nearby, gradually attaching to his sons.

Love dissolves fear. Our love gently dissolved his fears and the projection of his fears onto us. Eventually we were married after my first year of medical school, when Carole was graduated from college. My father came to love Carole as a daughter, and he blessed our marriage.

When your intuitions, your gut-feelings, your spiritual heart all know beyond any doubt, do not be swayed by the fear-based arguments of others. Sometimes meaning well, and sometimes not, they might lead you far astray from your joy.

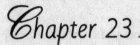

Chapter 23 _____

It is not more surprising to be born twice than once;
everything in nature is resurrection.

VOLTAIRE

℘lizabeth called me from Boston. She had extended her vacation. Pedro had returned from London immediately after his business there was concluded. He was in Boston, too, to be with Elizabeth. They were already falling in love.

They had begun to compare their experiences of past lives, which they both remembered vividly. They were discovering each other, once again.

"He really is special," she commented.

"So are you," I reminded her.

Following my experiences with Elizabeth and Pedro, my practice has taken an indescribably beautiful leap into the mystical and magical. When I conduct large workshops in which each participant is presented with the opportunity to experience deeply relaxed and hypnotic states, the frequency of magical events rises dramatically.

The range of experiences extends far beyond past lives

165

and reincarnation. Beautiful spiritual and mystical events emerge frequently and with life-transforming power. I have been blessed to help facilitate these events. Here is what happened in one two-week span.

A reporter for a local newspaper attended a weekend series of seminars and workshops in Boston. She wrote the following.

Many people in Weiss' past-life regression workshops related profound emotional and spiritual experiences. One exercise was particularly dramatic.

Weiss had the lights turned down and asked everyone in the room to find a partner. He directed the pairs to look into each other's faces for several minutes while he guided the meditation with his voice.

When the exercise was over, two women who had never met shared that they'd each seen themselves as the other's sister.

One woman said she kept seeing a nun in her partner's face. When she told her partner this, the woman replied that in the previous day's session she'd had a past-life memory in which she was a nun.

Most amazing was a local woman who saw in her partner's face her nineteen and one half year old brother who'd been killed in World War II. Her partner was a younger woman from Wisconsin who explained that she had also had a past life memory the day before; that of being a nineteen-and-a-half-year-old man in army boots and fatigues, killed in a war that had to be earlier than Viet Nam. The healing experienced by the local woman was palpable in the room.

"Love dissolves anger," said Weiss. "That's the spiritual part. Valium doesn't do it. Prozac doesn't do it."

And love heals grief.

The brilliant psychotherapist, cellular biologist, and author, Dr. Joan Borysenko, was standing next to me, responding to my keynote address, "Spiritual Implications of Past-Life Therapy," given at the Boston conference.

Her blue eyes danced as she related a ten-year-old story. At that time, she was a highly respected researcher on the faculty of Harvard Medical School. During a conference on nutrition at a Boston hotel, at which Joan was one of the speakers, she happened to run into her boss, who was attending a medical conference at the same hotel. He was surprised to see her there.

Back at work, her boss threatened her. If she ever again lent the name of Harvard University to such a frivolous affair as a nutrition conference, she would not be working at Harvard anymore.

Times have changed enormously since then, even at Harvard. Not only is nutrition now a mainstream area of teaching and research, but some faculty members at Harvard are confirming and expanding on my work with past-life regression therapy.

The next weekend I conducted a two-day seminar in San Juan, Puerto Rico. Nearly five hundred people attended, and again there was magic. Many people experienced early-childhood, in-utero, and past-life memories. One participant, a forensic psychiatrist well respected in Puerto Rico, experienced even more.

During a guided meditation on the second day of the conference, his inner eye perceived the shadowy figure of a young woman. She approached him.

"Tell them I am well," she directed him. "Tell them Natasha is well."

The psychiatrist felt "very silly" as he related his experience to the entire group. After all, he knew nobody named Natasha. The name itself is a rarity in Puerto Rico. And the message related by the ghostlike girl had no connection to anything happening in the conference or in his personal life.

"Does the message have any meaning to anybody here?" the psychiatrist asked the audience.

Suddenly a woman screamed in the back of the auditorium. "My daughter, my daughter!"

Her daughter, who had died suddenly in her twenties, only six months before, was named Ana Natalia. Her mother, and only her mother, called her Natasha.

The psychiatrist had never met nor heard of Natasha or her mother. He was as unnerved by this extraordinary experience as was the mother. When both had regained their composure, Natasha's mother showed him a photo of her daughter. The psychiatrist again grew pale. This was the same young woman whose shadowy figure had approached him with her amazing message.

The next weekend I led a conference in Mexico City. Once again, wonderful magic was breaking out all around me. The familiar arms-turning-to-gooseflesh feeling was happening with stunning regularity.

After a meditation, a woman in the audience began to cry happily. She had just experienced a past-life memory in which her current husband was her son. She had been a male in a medieval lifetime, and she, the father, had abandoned him. In this present life, her husband has always feared that she would leave him. This fear had no rational basis in the current life. She had never even threatened to leave him. She reassured him constantly, but his overwhelming insecurity devastated his life and was poisoning the relationship.

Now she understood the real source of her husband's dread. She rushed to telephone him with the answer and with her reassurance that she would never leave him again.

Relationships can sometimes heal incredibly fast.

At the end of the seminar's second day, as I was signing books, a woman came through the line, crying softly.

"Thank you so much!" she whispered as she took my hand. "You don't know what you have done for me!

"I've had terrible pains in my upper back for the past ten years. I've been to doctors here, in Houston, and Los Angeles. Nobody has been able to help me, and I've suffered terribly. In the past-life regression yesterday, I saw myself as a soldier being stabbed in the back, just below the neck. Just where my pain is. The pain disappeared, for the first time in *ten years*, and it's still gone!" She was so happy she could not stop smiling and crying.

Lately I've been telling people that regression therapy can take weeks or months to work, that they should not get discouraged because the process seems to be going slowly. This lady reminded me that progress can also be unbelievably rapid.

As she walked away, I wondered what other miracles the future would bring.

The more I see my patients and workshop participants recalling memories of their past lives, and the more I witness their magical and mystical experiences, the more

I am reminded that the concept of reincarnation is only a bridge.

The therapeutic results of walking over this bridge are beyond question. People get better, even if they don't believe in past lives. The belief of the therapist isn't important either. Memories are elicited and symptoms resolve.

So many people, however, become fixated on the bridge rather than finding what lies beyond. They obsess about minor details, names, historical accuracies. Their whole focus is on discovering as many details from as many past lives as they can.

They are missing the forest for the trees. Reincarnation is a bridge to greater knowledge, wisdom, and understanding. It reminds us of what we take with us and what we do not, of why we are here and of what we need to accomplish in order to move on. It reminds us of the incredible guidance and help along the way, and of our loved ones returning with us to share our steps and to ease our burdens.

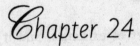

Chapter 24 _____

Over the years, many of my patients have become my teachers. They constantly bring me gifts of their stories and experiences, gifts of their knowledge and spiritual understanding. Some have become my dear friends, sharing their lives as well as their gifts.

Years ago, before *Many Lives, Many Masters* was published but after my work with Catherine and dozens of subsequent regression patients, a patient brought in two messages for me. She had received the messages in dreams and wrote them down upon awakening. They came from Philo, a person I, too, had seen in dreams and later identified in my first book. This patient did not know about my dream experiences. The "coincidence" of the same name was interesting.

Did the messages come from her subconscious mind? From an outside source, such as Philo? From a forgotten memory of something she had read or heard earlier in her life? Perhaps it does not matter. To paraphrase my daughter, Amy: "Real is a matter of existence, and it existed in her mind." My messages from Philo also spoke of the mind.

> To BLW. The mind in each of us can comprehend all other things but is unable to know itself. For let it say what it is and whence, whether it is spirit or blood or fire or some other substance or only so much, whether it is corporeal or incorporeal.
>
> We are ignorant of when the soul enters the body. You've done good work in guiding beings to recognize that moment. It is a good beginning.
>
> Your friend,
>
> Philo

The other message came a week later and dealt with the nature of God.

> To BLW. We must remember, too, that the transcendent Being is the only cause, the father and the creator of the universe. That he fills all things not with His thought only but with His essence.
>
> His essence is not exhausted in the universe. He is above it and beyond.
>
> We may say that only His powers are in the universe. But while He is above His powers, He includes them. What they do, He does *through them*.
>
> Now they are visible, working in the world. From their activity we get a clue to the nature of God.
>
> Ideés Philo

I can perceive great truths in these words, whatever their source.

I have met famous psychics and mediums, priests and gurus, and I have learned many things from them. Some are incredibly talented, and some are not.

It has become clear to me that there is no direct correlation between psychic abilities and level of spiritual evolution. I remember a conversation I had with Edgar Mitchell, the well-known astronaut and researcher of paranormal phenomena. In his laboratory, Edgar had studied a famous psychic who could affect energies and by doing so could move a compass point through a magnetic field and even move objects by the power of his mind, a phenomenon known as telekinesis. Despite these obviously advanced psychic abilities, Edgar noticed that the character and personality of this psychic were definitely not consistent with a high level of spiritual awareness. He was the first to point out to me that psychic abilities and spiritual development are not necessarily connected.

I believe that the psychic abilities of some people increase as they progress spiritually, as they become more and more aware. This is more of an incidental acquisition rather than an essential step. One's ego should not become inflated merely because the level of one's psychic abilities increases. The goal is to learn about love and compassion, about goodness and charity, not about becoming a famous psychic.

Even therapists can become extremely psychic, if they allow it, while working with their patients. Sometimes I can pick up psychic impressions, intuitive knowledge, or even physical impressions relating to the patient sitting in the comfortable chair across from me.

A few years ago I treated a young Jewish woman who was extremely despondent. She was feeling out of place, feeling that somehow she was in the wrong family. The center of both of my palms began to ache with a sharp pain as I talked to her, and I couldn't figure out why. I looked at the arms of my leather chair. There was no break in the leather, no sharp edges, no reason for this kind of pain. Yet it was getting even more severe and beginning to sting and to burn. I looked at my hands, and I could see no marks or impressions, no cuts, no reason for this.

Then a thought appeared suddenly in my mind: This is like being crucified. I decided to ask her what this meant. "What does the crucifixion mean to you? Do you have some connection with Jesus?" She just looked at me, her face blanching. She had been secretly going to church since she was eight years old. She had never told her parents about this feeling that she was really Catholic.

This sensation in my hands and the connection we had made were able to help my patient break the logjam of her life and to know that she was not crazy, she was not bizarre, that her feelings had a basis in reality. She began, finally, to understand and to heal. Eventually we found a powerful past life she had experienced in Palestine two thousand years ago.

We are all psychics, and we are all gurus. We have merely forgotten.

A patient asked me about Sai Baba, a great holy man in India. Is he an avatar, a divine incarnation, a descent of deity to earth in incarnate form?

"I don't know," I replied, "but in some sense, aren't we all?"

We are all gods. God is within us. We should not be distracted by psychic abilities, for these are merely sign-posts along the way. We need to express our divinity and our love by good deeds, by service.

Perhaps no one should be anyone else's guru for longer than a month or two. Repeated trips to India are not necessary since the real journey lies within.

There are distinct benefits to having one's own tran-scendent experiences, to begin opening up to the realiza-tion of the divine, to the understanding that life is so much more than meets the eye. Oftentimes you don't believe it if you don't see it.

Our path is an inward one. This is the more difficult path, the more painful journey. We bear the responsibility for our own learning. This responsibility cannot be exter-nalized and dumped on someone else, on some guru.

The kingdom of God is within you.

Epilogue

*I am certain that I have been here as I am now a
thousand times before, and I hope to return a thousand
times.*

GOETHE

From time to time, I hear from Elizabeth and Pedro.
They are happily married now and live in Mexico, where
Pedro has become involved in politics in addition to his
businesses. Elizabeth cares for their beautiful little girl,
who has long brown hair and loves picking flowers from
their garden and chasing the butterflies that flutter around
her.

"Thank you for everything," Elizabeth wrote recently.
"We are so happy, and we owe so much of it to you."

I don't believe they owe me anything. I don't believe
in coincidences. I helped them to meet, but they would
have met anyway, even without me. That's how destiny
works.

When allowed to flow freely, love overcomes all obstacles.

Dr. Weiss maintains a private clinic in Miami, Florida, where he has expanded his offices to include well-trained and highly experienced psychologists and social workers who also use regression therapy in their work. In addition, Dr. Weiss conducts seminars and experiential workshops nationally and internationally as well as training programs for professionals. He has recorded a series of audiotapes in which he helps you discover and learn techniques of meditation, healing, deep relaxation, regression, and other visualization exercises.

For more information, please contact:

The Weiss Institute
PO Box 560788
Miami, Florida 33256-0788, USA
Phone: (001) 305 598-8151
Fax: (001) 305 598-4009
Website: www.brianweiss.com

Also by Dr Brian Weiss:

SAME SOUL, MANY BODIES

Dr Brian Weiss

In this astounding and groundbreaking book, Dr Brian Weiss reveals
how our future lives can transform us in the present. We have all lived
past lives. All of us will live future ones. What we do in this life will
influence our lives to come as we evolve towards immortality.

Dr Brian Weiss has not only regressed all of his patients into the past,
but also progressed them into the future. He has discovered that our
futures are variable and the choices we make now will determine the
quality of our lives when we return. Using dozens of case histories, Dr
Weiss demonstrates the therapeutic benefits of progression therapy to
bring patients more peace, joy and healing, just as he has shown that
journeys into our past lives can cure physical or
emotional wounds in the present.

978-0-7499-2541-3